Radical Presence

Radical Presence

TEACHING AS CONTEMPLATIVE PRACTICE

Mary Rose O'Reilley

BOYNTON/COOK PUBLISHERS
HEINEMANN
PORTSMOUTH, NH

Boynton/Cook Publishers, Inc.
A subsidiary of Reed Elsevier Inc.
361 Hanover Street
Portsmouth, NH 03801–3912

Offices and agents throughout the world

The author and publisher thank those who generously gave permission to reprint borrowed material:
"Lying in a Hammock at William Duffy's Farm in Pine Island, Minnesota" by James Wright from *The Branch Will Not Break* © 1963 by James Wright, Wesleyan University Press by permission of University Press of New England.

Portions of "An Experiment in Friendship" originally appeared as "Deep Listening: An Experimental Friendship" by Mary Rose O'Reilley. In *Weavings*, Vol. IX, No. 3 (May/June 1994). Copyright 1994 by The Upper Room.

"Nourishing the Prophetic Vision" was originally published in *Community College Humanities Association Review*, Vol. 16 (December 1995). Reprinted by permission of Community College Humanities Association.

Library of Congress Cataloging-in-Publication Data
O'Reilley, Mary Rose.
    Radical presence : teaching as contemplative practice / Mary Rose O'Reilley ;
    foreword by Parker J. Palmer.
        p.   cm.
    Includes bibliographical references.
    ISBN: 0-86709-427-3
    1. Teaching—Philosophy. 2. Education—Philosophy. 3. Thought and thinking. I. Title.
LB1025.3.074 1998
370'.1—dc21   97-44855
                                            CIP

Acquisitions editor: Scott Mahler
Production editor: Elizabeth Valway
Cover designer: Jenny Jensen Greenleaf
Manufacturing coordinator: Louise Richardson

Printed in the United States of America on acid-free paper
02 01 00   DA   4 5

For Mom and Peggy, with love.
In memory of my father.

Contents

Foreword

TEACHING IS A DIFFICULT THING TO DO, AND MOST OF US WHO teach know how rarely we do it well. *Writing* well about teaching is more difficult still. But Mary Rose O'Reilley writes so beautifully about this occult art—writes with such honesty, grittiness, lyricism, and wit—that, early on in reading her manuscript, I began to suspect that this book might help me become a better teacher. Once I finished the book, I knew for a fact that it would help me, and all who read it, become better teachers—if we receive it in the same openhearted way it was written.

We might even become better people, for this book is about our lives as well as our work. The "secrets" of good teaching are the same as the secrets of good living: seeing one's self without blinking, offering hospitality to the alien other, having compassion for suffering, speaking truth to power, being present and being real. These are secrets hidden in plain sight. But in an age that puts more faith in the powers of technique than in the powers of the human heart, it takes the clear sight and courage of someone like Mary Rose O'Reilley to call "secrets" of this sort to our attention.

I do not know how our culture managed to drift so far from its human moorings, to a lost and lonely place where "tips, tricks, and techniques" have become the commonest words in the literature about everything we do—from teaching to raising children to making love. But I do know that we must rescue teaching (and loving) from such gimmickry and manipulation, because teaching-and-learning at its best is one of the most ancient and elemental of all human exchanges. It has been going on ever since our primordial progenitors tried to pass the good news about fire.

Tips, tricks, and techniques are not the heart of education—fire is. I mean finding light in the darkness, staying warm in a cold world, avoiding being burned if you can, and knowing what brings healing if you cannot. That is the knowledge that our students really want, and that is the knowledge we owe them. Not merely the facts, not merely the theories, but a deep knowing of what it means to kindle the gift of life in ourselves, in others, and in the world.

Of course, this approach to teaching and learning not only takes us beyond technique, it also takes us onto the slippery slope of spirituality in education. It *is* a slippery slope—ask Copernicus or Galileo. But secularism is slippery too, and we have just about reached the bottom of the secular slide. There is no religiously induced bias or bigotry or blindness in education that cannot, and has not, been matched by secular sources. More important, there is a deep yearning among teachers and students today—a yearning for embodied meaning—that will be fulfilled only as education embraces the fact that what is inward and invisible is at least as important as what is outward and empirical.

Mary Rose O'Reilley is wonderfully well suited, by struggle and sensibility, to lead us through the perils and promise of the spiritual realm: what better guide could we have than someone whose lineage is Catholic-Quaker-Buddhist? Her spirituality is grounded not in doctrine or dogma, but in the place where all debates are resolved, where everyone and everything is equal, the place from which all life came and to which it will return: the great silence.

There is an old Quaker saying I have always loved: "Don't speak unless you can improve upon the silence." It is an intimidating counsel if taken literally, but that is not how it is meant. It simply reminds us that the words we speak about important things are always partial and penultimate, so they must be chosen with care and abandon—care because we want to tell the truth, abandon because the truth can never be told as long as we are in tight control. "Tell the truth but tell it slant," said Emily Dickinson, and this book shows what powerful advice that is.

The genius of the book you are about to read is that Mary Rose O'Reilley chooses her words with care-filled abandon: she takes us deep and she takes us by surprise. Read this book with your mind descended into your heart, and it will draw you, as it drew me, into a silent and reflective space where we can practice listening, being present, receiving others, and being truthful—the secrets at the heart of teaching, and living, well.

Parker J. Palmer, Ph.D.
Author of *The Courage to Teach: Exploring the Inner Landscape of a Teacher's Life* (San Francisco: Jossey-Bass, 1998).

Preface

TO TALK ABOUT THE SPIRITUALITY OF ONE'S WORK MAY SUGGEST that one has reached some stage of enlightenment: in my case, that's not true. In fact I would not venture upon such a formidable topic without recalling Virginia Woolf's remark that, in real life, Charlotte Brontë was a terrible governess, second only to Emily. My colleagues and students know all about my struggles as a teacher. I write simply as one taking notes on the inner life of great teaching I've witnessed, most often in my department at the University of St. Thomas, St. Paul, Minnesota. I'm indebted to my colleague Michael Mikolajczak for this quotation from Hans Urs von Balthasar: "Truth is symphonic." My own orchestra station is typically somewhere among the second violins, and I offer these few notes in harmony (I hope) with the stronger players. It's a song all of us know—I've merely tried to write it down.

Mary Rose O'Reilley

Acknowledgments

MUCH OF WHAT'S WRITTEN HERE CAME OUT OF SOMEONE'S request or assignment. Early versions were tried out in many venues, among them the Southwestern Regional Conference of the Community College Humanities Association, Colorado Springs, Colorado; Pendle Hill Center for Study and Contemplation, Wallingford, Pennsylvania; Richland College, Dallas, Texas; Luther College, Decorah, Iowa; Yavapai College, Prescott, Arizona; St. Olaf College, Northfield, Minnesota; River Falls State University, River Falls, Wisconsin; North Carolina (Conservative) Yearly Meeting of the Society of Friends; Friends Association for Higher Education Conference, Haverford College, Haverford, Pennsylvania; and the Bluffton College Peace Studies Conference, Bluffton, Indiana. I would like to thank my colleagues at those institutions for their hospitality and for raising the issues; I'm particularly grateful to Nancy K. Barry, Sandra Desjardins, Jim Farrell, Jeff Gundy, Mike Heller, Bob and Carol Passmore, Donn Rawlings and Elaine Sullivan.

I would also like to thank Mary Louise Buley-Meissner, Mary McCaslin Thompson, and Elizabeth Bachrach Tan who requested the chapter titled "Love Calls Us to the Things of This World" for a project they were working on, and whose painstaking editorial suggestions gave coherent direction not only to that chapter but to much of what came later.

As I was in the delicate stages of finishing the book, my colleagues at St. Thomas, Michael Mikolajczak and Robert K. Miller, offered excellent suggestions and, above all, that mysterious resonance fiddlers need to keep playing.

Finally, I thank my teachers Peter Elbow, Parker Palmer, and Thich N'hat Hanh.

1

To Teach Is to Create a Space

THE LANGUAGE OF COMMERCE DOMINATES MODERN LIFE.
Consequently, the metaphors that inform professional culture
today reflect a dialect of buying and selling and trading in hog
futures. It's not uncommon for us teachers to hear about the
"packaging" of programs and ideas, how to position our "prod-
uct" in the educational "market." The mercantile chant swells with
each capital campaign, each new edition of the catalogue, or even
the enthusiasm of opening convocation. Students are the desig-
nated "consumers" in this mall of ideas, and what that makes us
teachers I can't bear to imagine: the spector of Willie Loman haul-
ing his sample cases haunts my imagination. I think we should
challenge this dialect, because it insults the sacredness of our calling. We deal with what *can't* be bought: in fact, I think the per-
vasiveness of this shabby rhetoric reflects an attempt by the
mysterious forces that drive consumer culture to annihilate the
spirituality of our work—to annihilate it out of fear, because
nothing is so scary and puzzling as a person who can't be bought
or a pearl with no price tag.

Parker Palmer, who leads workshops on teaching and learning around the country, suggests a different universe of possibility when he says, "To teach is to create a space . . ." These are rev-
olutionary words, because most of us think in terms of filling a
space: filling the number of minutes between the beginning and
end of class, filling the student's notebook, filling the student's
head. These are responsible gestures, sanctioned by custom, and I
would not ask us to abolish our generous practice of feeding students from a rich banquet of culture. But, as with so many habit-
ual actions, it's useful to ask ourselves, "What if we did the opposite?" What if, instead of feeding, we were to honor the hunger
with which our students come to school? What if, instead of cook-
ing up the cultural menu, we inquired what kind of loaves and

1

fishes might be available in the room? What if we took away their notebooks? What would be happening in the classroom if *nothing* were happening?

These questions arise for me as I think about Parker Palmer's comment. Others might frame a different poetics of space. Such anti-questions pique my interest, questions bred of Zen practice, questions that follow, in my own formation, from the Quaker principle that there is that of the divine spirit in everyone. What would it mean to take such an idea seriously? Why, we would have to *create a space*, as, in my parochial school days, we children were asked to leave room on the bench for our guardian angels.

Most of us believe, at some level, that what happens in the classroom is caused by the teacher. In reality, we cause or control very little. To "create a space" acknowledges both our sphere of responsibility and our lack of control. The idea of filling students, well-intentioned and nurturing as it may be, rests on the conviction that we know what they need, that their hunger is like our own, or something like the hunger we felt in college. This may not be true. How do we find out? Probably by keeping quiet much more than we have ever imagined possible, and by listening more astutely than we have before, even if we have listened long and hard. We plan lessons with a notion of what students need. But here is Jim, who unexpectedly needs to love that sentimental poem; here is Sylvia, whose block about math holds her together while her spirit heals some painful abuse. Respect the blocks. Respect the stutter. We know so little about what's really going on. What seem to be mistakes are often gifts of the spirit. Years ago, when I was a young teacher, some new bombing raid in Cambodia brought me to tears in English 101—what shame I felt about losing my professional demeanor. And yet, one student wrote on his final evaluation, "The best thing I learned in this class is that tears are sometimes appropriate."

It's good to remember, in general, that things may be the opposite—or at least a few degrees off—of what our enculturation leads us to expect. If we can even begin to hold this idea in mind, we are on the road to deconditioning ourselves and welcoming new vistas of possibility. I went to a Native American powwow once that was supposed to start at ten P.M. It got going around two in the morning. The delay left me exhausted and crabby.

"What is it about Native Americans and the clock?" I wanted to know.

"What is it about Anglos and the clock?" replied my Ojibwe friend. "We think it is a sin to start before the spirit is present."

Class starts at 8:15. Is the spirit present? If not, keep waiting.

In the chapters that follow, I'm asking what might happen if we try to frame the central questions of our discipline as spiritual questions, and to deal with them in the light of our spiritual understanding. The traditions

(Catholic, Quaker, and Buddhist) that have nurtured me have in common the ground of contemplation and an educational system that grows out of contemplation and returns to it for nurturance. The basis of my remarks here will not be religious, however, but pedagogical. I would like to ask what spaces we can create in the classroom that will allow students freedom to nourish an inner life. Theorists such as Robert Coles and Edward Robinson have explored the idea, should a theoretical foundation be needed, that students *have* an inner life and that its authority is central to understanding cognitive development. Teaching, then, has much in common with the ancient art of spiritual guidance. I see my colleagues practicing this patient discernment as seriously as any Zen master, though they may call it simply draft conferencing. These essays, these *tries* our students make, are forays into secret, mysterious inner space, for them and for us.

Now, all things being equal, certain things help us to live a contemplative life and others do not. Silence helps. How can we make a space for it in the classroom? Mindfulness helps: the Buddhist practice of simply *being there*, with a very precise and focused attention, listening, watching. Not being somewhere else, answering some question that hasn't been asked. Being attentive even, as the Sufi practice has it, for those who are not capable of being attentive themselves.

Some pedagogical practices crush the soul; most of us have suffered their bruising force. Others allow the spirit to come home: to self, to community, and to the revelations of reality. What follows is my own try at articulating a space in which teacher and student can practice this radical presence.

2

"Love Calls Us to the Things of This World"

I BECAME SERIOUSLY INTERESTED IN THE CONTEMPLATIVE vocation—though I didn't know the name of what I was interested in—at about the age of seven, when I covered a card table in my bedroom with a blanket, put a nightlight inside (it was a big conch shell with a bulb in it that my grandparents had brought me from Florida), and retired to read and think. Over the years, my doctrinal allegiances have shifted and changed, though the commitment to the inner life retains its claim. If someone asks about my spiritual formation, I find I must divide the question physiologically, top down. I have a Buddhist mind, or no-mind, at least when I practice Zen successfully. Or, since it is not good Zen to talk about practicing successfully, when I am practicing faithfully. Tumbling down the chakras: I have a Catholic heart. I belong to a parish. I go to Mass. I have a card in my wallet that says, "I am a radical Catholic; in case of accident please call Daniel Berrigan." And—some would say "but"—I also belong to a Quaker meeting. To conclude the physiological metaphor, you might say I have a Quaker backside, which I position conscientiously on a folding chair at Twin Cities Friends Meeting once a week. I sit there with my Catholic heart and my Buddhist mind, trying to achieve consensus of my inner committee. ("But where will we hold your wake?" is a question that worries my Catholic relatives.)

It makes for messy bookkeeping, this triple allegiance, but for me it works because the contemplative ground of all spiritual experience is the same. As the Quaker tradition puts it, the way opens in silence: "Lying down in the Lamb's patience," Isaac Penington wrote in 1678 (1984, 155). Contemplative silence might not be attractive to everyone (and restless Quakers will attest that

4

it is not for *anyone* all the time). Still, I do not think contemplation is some kind of spiritual feat; I think it is a dimension of being human—though one from which modern life often distracts us—and that's why I think it's appropriate to talk about the contemplative dimensions of teaching. By nature, we crave food and love and silence. So, though we may try to avoid becoming contemplatives, in a sense we are *already there.* The Judeo-Christian tradition tells us that, no matter our degree of avoidance, we are objects of transcendent longing. As Julian of Norwich puts it, "In this endless love we are led and protected by God and we never shall be lost" (1978, 284).

We may, of course, resist the passions of spirit. Indeed, I think that resistance is itself a spiritual process, a way of pacing ourselves so that growth and healing occur in all the structures of the human organism concurrently. It is natural to resist, and it is natural at a certain point to stop resisting, and when we stop resisting that will be the time to look for a bench to sit on and keep quiet.

One good reason to resist, to utter relentlessly the "mortal no" of Wallace Stevens (1971), is that so many of us have been scarred by pseudo-spiritual chicanery of one kind or another. That is why I need to address one more issue before I talk about contemplative practice in the classroom: the concept of "faith" or "belief" that is implicit here. "You are not really one of us," certain religious people will say to me. "You are merely sitting on a bench. You have declared no *faith.* Or, worse yet, you are babbling about *three* allegiances—which shows a sloppy indecision, and no doubt, a disinclination to pay pew rent or contribute to the building fund." Well, these objections are well founded. I must admit that, when people start to talk about "faith," I take a trip into the Zen quarters of my mind, because Zen people merely talk about "practice" and do not address issues of what an individual believes. No matter what theological quandary we used to bring to my Zen teacher, he would respond with a sympathetic cluck and the simple question, "Yes, but are you practicing?" Are you sitting zazen, putting in your time on the zafu (or *snafu,* as we despairing Western students came to call it). The Zen idea is that spiritual observance teaches us to be spiritual. Practice teaches us what we seek to know and reveals what each one needs to learn about the nature of spirit. Whatever else goes on in a Zen community—potlucks, dating, counselling, theologizing—is far from the point. The point is to keep the prayer hall open.

Quakerism, similarly, attempts to discern "the light within"—the inner teacher who leads each of us on an appropriate path. And this simple principle recurs in the great contemplative literature of all traditions. The Jesuit spiritual teacher Jean-Pierre de Caussade, for example, reminds us that when we are thirsty we do not read a book about thirst, we take a long drink (1975, 27). That's a definition of *practice.*

In commenting on the gulf between faith and knowledge, Carl Jung claimed the epistemological high ground: "I don't believe; I know." For my part, I don't know; I merely suspect (from the Latin *suspicere,* "to look up at"). And I want to talk about allowing space, in the classroom, for the suspicion to grow. I want to talk about keeping a kind of prayer hall open, so that each student will find what he or she needs. Under the mortal no, finally, lies "a passion for yes that has never been broken" (Stevens 1971, 258).

Let me return here to Parker Palmer's comment, "To teach is to create a space." For what, we wonder? Well, for whatever has to happen. The act of contemplation begins, for each of us, simply in creating a space. Of course one can go further than that, but for my part, I am still at step one. After twenty-five years of teaching, it takes all the courage I have to keep silence for a minute and a half after reading a poem aloud, or asking a question that heads us all for the depths of experience. A minute and a half of silence is, however pitiful, a space. Something can rush in, something we did not plan and cannot control; how each of us, students and teachers, experiences these "openings" (to use the Quaker term) will differ.

In the practical order, what are some ways we can introduce contemplative practice in the classroom? We must recognize, first, that to do so contradicts much traditional pedagogy. Many of us teachers are as scared of dead air in the classroom as any radio announcer in the studio. Partly it is a market analysis. As one of my friends, a Quaker teacher, puts it, "Quaker meetings are good, but in the classroom they are expensive."

Writing exercises, though, can create a spacious moment: at the beginning of class to find a spiritual center; in the middle, to brainstorm; and at the end, to reflect. "What's your gut reaction to today's reading?" we might begin. And later, as energy flags, we might pause to regroup and write privately on a question that has proved obstinate. But the final period of quiet is, in my experience, the most productive, surprising, and moving. "Write a moment and gather together your thoughts on today's discussion; come to some experience of closure," I sometimes say as we move into the last fifteen minutes of class. Five minutes later, one might suggest a final coda: "Does anyone wish to speak out of the silence? Share any final thoughts?"

The first time I issued this invitation—and it happened to be in the first week of a freshman course—I expected no takers, an early exit toward lunch. But a young man began, "I'd like to thank Jennifer for what she said. It took me right to the heart of the poem." Other students asked questions to be carried over to the next day, meditated on insights that had occurred to them—

and, again and again, thanked each other. A gentle closing. Students seem to thrive on such islands of quiet. The classroom, in today's multimedia culture, may be the only site of reflection in a student's day. Perhaps we teachers should respect that sacred space at least as much as we respect the tradition of Socratic dialogue.

But first we may have to overcome a few negative ideas about silence. In daily speech, the word silence often goes around with the word uncomfortable in front of it. Silence in relationships may be perceived as coldness, a state of nongiving. Then there is the Tillie Olsen silence, when you don't have a voice, when you are discounted, marginalized, standing there ironing. In the beginning, we have it on good authority, was the word.

It's hard to practice silence in the classroom without being overly precious or cute. It helps to talk about it, to explain a little about what you're doing, to redefine the classroom order a bit. This sounds more difficult than it really is. Students are used to code switching as they go from, say, a Spanish-speaking home to a logical-positivist philosophy class, and from there to sociology—with its empirical boundaries—to my class, where we do silence. This is how I put it in my syllabus:

> This course moves rather slowly and covers material in depth rather than breadth. Try to be patient with going back over material in silence and slow time. I don't like to talk all the time, or to hear other people talk all the time. I often have to sit quietly in order to come up with an answer or analysis; sometimes I have to write a little, and perhaps I will stop class to do that: or perhaps that is not stopping class, but continuing class in a different way. I think that if we proceed in this rather contemplative manner we can get to deeper understandings. This is not McSchool; there are no golden arches out front.

We talk about this statement on the first day of class; at the very least it serves as a consumer warning, and students who prefer the fast track can speed right off and drop the course.

If we allow enough quiet, a diversity of voices begins to be heard. Of course, this may be reason enough for some teachers to *avoid* allowing their students any reflective time. Reflection is the enemy of authoritarian conditioning. Some teachers who lecture constantly presume both consensus and understanding—or perhaps don't care if students disagree or misunderstand. If, by contrast, we talk, reflect, keep silence, and encourage multivocalism, our classrooms are going to be a lot more edgy and astonishing. Perhaps because I have considerable tolerance for chaos, I love W. B. Yeats' characterization of Incarnation as "the uncontrollable mystery" (1950, 124).

I often remember the phrase when students bring to light their wild and unpredictable responses to silent inner search.

My freshman literature students are, at the moment, reading the *Narrative of the Life of Frederick Douglass* and trying to make sense of Douglass' rapture in the presence of Sophia Auld, the woman who taught him to read. We have been calling this a "vision of Sophia"—wisdom. The freshmen are sitting and thinking about whether anyone has ever inspired them in this way.

Charlie sits quietly for awhile. Then he exclaims, "Rush Limbaugh!" and testifies ardently to the virtues of his hero. This makes me smile. It also amuses me when my students, hot from reading Thoreau, engage in civil disobedience on the opposite side of an issue than I might incline to. It seems good evidence that they are learning what they need to know, not filling their notebooks with the fruits of *my* spiritual journey. When students engage actively in reflection and response—merging in their inimitable way the contemplative and active vocations—they often take a direction we might not approve or affirm. Their inner teacher may speak differently from ours: surprise us, amuse us, instruct us, anger us. In such circumstances, we will *need* that closing dialectic of speech and silence: it constitutes a liturgy of assimilation and forgiveness.

Silence creates one kind of contemplative space. The practice of hospitality, in the Benedictine sense, defines another: "All guests who present themselves are to be welcomed as Christ," says the Rule of St. Benedict (Chittister 1990, 121). Hospitality defines a space for the visitor—the student—to be herself, because she is received graciously. Indeed, if real inner searching is going on, real multivocalism practiced, the transcendent disciplines of courtesy become essential to civil exchange. I mention this hospitality space, too, in the syllabus. I tell the students that I expect them to attend class regularly, and that I will try to receive them with unconditional presence. In making this small promise, I articulate a discipline for myself. I do not succeed at it very often, but I've found it, as all disciplines should be, a useful anchor in the midst of our turbulent days. Some of my colleagues are conscientious about getting to class early so that they are able to welcome their students; the more disorganized among us can specialize in graceful leave-taking.

Another daily ritual helps me to practice hospitality—and, as I get older, to simply remember names. I check attendance every day on three-by-five-inch cards, usually while people are quietly writing. On the first day of class, students write a lot of different things about themselves on these cards—what high school they went to, their major, their likes and dislikes, and their completion of a sentence beginning "I'm the one who . . ." So, every day, during this quiet five minutes, I can remember who each student is: the one from Chicago, the one who's majoring in plant pathology, the one who knows all of Sting's lyrics. Hospitality calls me to consider the singularity of each person, the diversity of needs. The discipline of presence requires me to *be there*, with my senses focused on the group at hand, listening rather than thinking about what I'm going to say—observing the students, the texts, and the sensory world of the classroom. This is harder than sitting zazen. In zazen, nobody talks back to you. Hospitality, by contrast, implies reception of the challenging and unfamiliar: that student with spiked hair who has written on her card, "I'm the one with tatoos all over my body." Joan Chittister, O.S.B., commenting on the Benedictine Rule, characterizes hospitality in terms of "the unbounded heart." "Benedictine spirituality," she goes on, "says that we must continue to beg the stranger to come into our lives because in the stranger may come the only honesty and insight we can get in our plastic worlds" (1990, 125).

I've spoken of *presence* as an aspect of hospitality; now I'd like to focus on it more specifically as a central premise of classroom "management." Presence, mindfulness, or—as I sometimes introduce it to students—*being awake* is an important Zen discipline, a dimension of contemplation, carried into the world. The Vietnamese Buddhist writer Thich N'hat Hanh explains it best in his commentary on the Sutra of Mindfulness, which he places in a context of humble household tasks:

> While washing dishes one should only be washing the dishes, which means that while washing the dishes one should be completely aware of the fact that one is washing the dishes. At first glance that might seem a little silly: why put so much stress on a simple thing? But that's precisely the point. The fact that I am standing there and washing this bowl is a wondrous reality, conscious of my presence, and conscious of my thoughts and actions. There's no way I can be tossed around mindlessly like a bottle slapped here and there on the waves. (4–5)

Such mindfulness may lead us (after an excruciating passage of time) to some degree of tranquility and clarity. It's a useful discipline to practice during two recurring and predictable crises of professional life: terror and boredom. As a first-year teacher, clinging to the lectern with white-knuckled hands, I wish I had known about mindfulness. What mostly preoccupied my attention in those days was an out-of-control mental voice-over: "What's going to happen next? What do they think of me? How should I respond?" By contrast, the experienced teacher has to deal with something much more like—doing the dishes. All sophomores wear baseball caps, you can't find anything new to say about comma splices, it's March and you have to teach *Moby Dick* one more time.

Tranquility is not precisely the goal of mindfulness practice—though many people begin to practice meditation in order to reduce stress. If we quiet ourselves, perhaps we can calm the mental chatter that makes us hostile, angry, and depressed. (Many spiritual writers have pointed out in different ways that we are the victims not of what happens to us, but of what we think about what happens to us.) The practice of mindfulness allows us a chance, at least, of seeing the pure data. It releases us from inner babble, shortcuts projection, and shuts down the mental movies that take up most of our day with fretting about what *I said* and *he said* and *he means* and *they might* and *I should*: all very tempting and amusing, but none of it, for the contemplative, *true*. What, by contrast, is true?

Let me answer (partially) with a sentence written by one of my advanced writing students: "I see that what we call evergreens are actually different colors of green." When I read that sentence I let out a happy yip. She has noticed something. It's sometimes hard to get students to notice anything at all. In this particular class, we have been reading Loren Eiseley and Annie Dillard, and I have asked students to do an exercise called "Writing in the Woods," which I introduce this way:

> For this exercise, I'd like you to, in Thoreau's phrase, "live as deliberately as Nature" for at least twenty minutes. Go someplace out of doors. Sit quietly and observe whatever comes into view. At the end of that time, write about the experience, taking any direction in the writing that occurs to you. It's important not to bring an agenda to this quiet sitting. Even though the writers we've been reading seem to come back from the woods with the Big Ideas, don't go questing for this kind of game. The Navaho people, I'm told, train their children to go out into nature and memorize what's given. I'll put one constraint on this exercise, just for fun: you have to sit or stand still. No walking the dog. No playing football. Dress warmly!

This particular class day, I have sent my class to the woods near campus, on a freezing cold day, and asked them to *be awake* for ten minutes. "I see that what we call evergreens are actually different colors of green," she tells us. Wonderful.

My son, who was studying psychology for awhile in a Buddhist context, told me about a Japanese psychiatrist who never talks to the patients in his hospital. Instead, he asks them to write daily journals and put them outside their rooms every day. He reads them, and when they write a single observation about the external world, such as "I see that what we call evergreens are actually different colors," he smiles. After awhile his patients seem to get well.

Maybe we can keep our students from getting sick. Today's writing assignment: draw the shape of a crow as it would look if it were flying over you. Nobody can. Well, that's a hard one, but if you cannot do it today, surely you will be able to do it tomorrow—because you will have done some research. Tell me, then, something very precise and concrete that you saw today in the external world. Quick now, no peeking. OK, peek. A yellow sneaker. That's grand. So much depends on it.

This moment is the only moment, this sneaker the only sneaker. As Annie Dillard put it in one of her more ecstatic moments in a writing class: "Is this what we live for? I thought; is this the only final beauty: the color of any skin in any light, and living, human eyes?"(1988, 151). The writer's moment—Buddhism aside, belief aside—is Now. Here is James Wright's moment:

> Over my head, I see the bronze butterfly,
> Asleep on the black trunk,
> Blowing like a leaf in green shadow.
> Down the ravine behind the empty house,
> The cowbells follow one another
> Into the distances of the afternoon. (1961, 16)

One of the many things I learned from the Buddhist writer Natalie Goldberg was how to help students pay attention to material like this. Read it aloud, she advises, and then "do a recall." What color was the butterfly? The trunk? The shadow? Where is the empty house? To what moments was the writer awake?

And as students read their own work to each other, we can ask them to recall. When was the writer awake? Do you remember *anything*? (If not, that tells us something about the piece—or about the quality of the listening.) Were there trees, or evergreens, or *blue spruce*? One of my advanced writing students this semester wrote a deeply felt, but rather generic, piece on the death of his father. Another student gently commented: "Jason, I'd like to come away with a better sense of who your father was, how he's different from my dad." Jason returned with a funny piece on a trip he took to the cabin with his seventy-three-year-old father. He never mentioned death, but gave us instead the details of packing the car, the blankets, "Barbie-doll pink, fuzzy like a bad crew cut." He gave us what his father wanted in the cooler: "Sauerkraut, pickles, loaf of bread, that blue container, a can of carnation milk, jam, no not that jam, the other one."

Being awake, then, is good writing practice. It leads to those prized concrete details. What does it have to do with spirituality? I'm not sure; I suspect, everything. I savor, without really understanding it, merely the title of Richard Wilbur's poem, quoted from St. Augustine: "Love Calls Us to the Things of This World"(1988, 233). Buddhism takes me to the edge; I'm too dense to go beyond. I long to go deeper into Wilbur's poem, through the laundry to the angels. There is a big difference between contemplative prayer and merely sitting under a card table with a blanket over your head. But sitting is a start.

Precise details open a window in the spaces where spirit abides and plays; our attentiveness to them measures the extent to which we are present. This semester I was working on memorizing Basho's famous poem "Furike ya" in honor of a Japanese visitor. And I was begging her—Yuki was my guest's name—to tell me what the poem means. A pond? A frog jumps? Silence returns? She covered her mouth with her hands and laughed (this being Yuki's characteristic response to most of my bumbling questions). "Much more," she told me.

Much more. The most unsophisticated Japanese schoolchild (who will have much of Basho by heart) has, I think, a respect for the hermeneutics of silence that we Westerners can scarcely approach.

It may seem as though I'm advocating an anti-intellectual approach here, a writer's universe made up of cows and tennis shoes and spruce trees with no thread of coherence among disparate bits of flotsam. This would not be a spiritual position, but, indeed, an anti-spiritual one: it would be the *nada* of doctrinaire modernism rather than the *nada* of apophatic mysticism. Let us return to Wright's poem, which would not be so good a poem without its cognitive resolution:

> To my right,
> In a field of sunlight between two pines,
> The droppings of last year's horses
> Blaze up into golden stones.
> I lean back, as the evening darkens and comes on.
> A chicken hawk floats over, looking for home.
> I have wasted my life.

Without the last line, it would not be so good an *American* poem, certainly. We do not like to sit long on the edge of silence. We like our little bites of meaning to take home. Anyway, it's impossible to practice pure attention all day long; the Zen tradition advocates it primarily as a corrective to the overwhelming tendency to dwell only in the mental world, chattering to ourselves like so many cockatoos without considering that there might even be an alternative.

I have described the practice of mindfulness mostly in Zen terms, because Zen language, in the Minnesota classrooms where I range, doesn't carry much baggage. By the same token, if I were teaching in Japan, perhaps I'd use the language of Thérèse of Lisieux: "If I did not simply live from one moment to the next, it would be impossible for me to keep my patience. I can see only the present. I forget the past and I take good care not to think about the future" (Beevers 1975, 16). I have chosen to use a diction, predominantly Buddhist, that is, for most Americans, value neutral. Someone who is trying to mediate specific religious values in the classroom, however, might see this as yet another evasion—indeed, another capitulation to silencing. For some of my fundamentalist or evangelical colleagues, the words themselves are counters inseparable from meaning: if you don't use the words, you don't affirm the reality. Such a reader would find my approach unacceptable.

Let me explain briefly my semantic feint, both in this essay and in the classroom. Over time, as we all know, words, phrases, and formulations that once rang and resonated with meaning ("*Theotokos!*" becoming an entirely sufficient war cry) lose connotation. They are devalued or, worse, they acquire a negative connotation (too many Sunday sermons on "stewardship" having preceded the passing of the hat). "God-talk" may become associated with childhood shaming, hypocrisy, or patriarchal oppression, and we lose our ability to hear and respond to any concept alive behind the patter.

I think the task of our time—and really, it is a poet's task—is to find words again that will mediate between spirit and matter. But I do not have time or skill enough to write that poem, so I'm trying to find a diction that unsettles the issues just enough to let us see them new. Perhaps it would be more accurate to call it not a value-neutral language but a value-seeking language. I'll take an example from what may be, for many of us, an uncongenial world of discourse: the New Age movement. When the New Age people talk about "visualization" it helps me to understand something of what Christians mean by prayer. They tell me that visualization changes the interior disposition of the visioner. Well, that's interesting. St. Teresa of Avila recommends intercessory prayer for the same reason. Perhaps I would not know that, or remember it, if the spiritual concept were not remediated for me in unfamiliar, perhaps even disquieting, language.

Another issue arises, of course, around inauthentic use of Buddhist language. I've tried to use this diction conscientiously, with a good history of practice and study. Eastern religious language in general is problematic for

American Buddhists because of the different conceptual frames of English and Japanese or Sanskrit. Let me simply conclude by saying that in my choice of words I have intended neither evasion, imprecision, or insult.

In trying to find neutral (or at least unbarnacled) language, I perhaps reveal some discomfort with the very idea of merging spiritual identity with professional life. Certainly, there are good reasons for keeping the two separate. I break silence on the issue because I know the longing we teachers feel to exist fully in the long stretch of identity: persons of a certain gender, ethnicity, race, sexual orientation, class, Myers-Briggs type, and—even—spirituality.

But this discomfort brings me to a final point. Once we begin to try to put spirituality and classroom practice together, let's not lose sight of some fundamental distinctions between them. Pedagogy emphasizes technique; spirituality addresses who we are. If silence, then, is not part of one's tradition, one might well hesitate to import it into one's pedagogy. I was a little unsettled by a remark I overheard one poet make to another, a Quaker: "I love the way you used silence. I'm going to do that in my next reading." The point is, we can't *use* silence, or we shouldn't. That would be like turning a sacrament or a pipe ceremony to our own end and profit. Pedagogical discussion brings us into a utilitarian world of what works and doesn't work; we habitually comment, as the lecturer drones on, "Oh, I tried that . . . I've done that . . . I've been there." But if we are on a path of being instead of a path of doing, those comments may not be appropriate.

Therefore, when we talk about teaching within a contemplative frame of reference, I think we should keep our prescriptions to a mimimum. I want to sketch the lines of a certain approach, but I don't want to trespass into another teacher's prayer hall. Good teachers—Jesus being a primary example—seldom tell you how to do whatever it is they do. Jesus was not an Arthur Murray dance teacher. He danced, he did not paint little feet on the floor, moving through the box waltz. That's why, approached in one way, it's so hard to figure out what he was teaching, and, approached in another, so easy. It's easy if you just dance and get the feeling of the process from within the process itself. So please don't try anything I've done and don't try anything that the Board of Education or the latest *College English* recommends: rather, lie down in the Lamb's patience and follow the deepest leadings of your own heart and your own tradition. Let methodology follow from the particular (this student, this hour, this blue spruce) rather than from the world of theory.

In fact, do what students are always telling each other to do—get a life. Permit yourself, that is, to stare out the window, to stay in bed, to have lunch, to have tea, to walk the dog, to fingerpaint, to listen to the texts you're teaching and face the consequences. Call it research. Sometimes I'm scared to do these quiet things because I might stumble on some data I didn't count on. In the contemplative mode, your life is always on the line. And if we define our classrooms as sacred space, we can expect that everything will be, at every moment, up for grabs, ". . . for there is no place at all"—says Rilke—"that isn't looking at you. You must change your life" (1981, 147).

3

An Experiment in Friendship

HENRI NOUWEN WROTE ABOUT

> how often we come out of a conversation, a social gathering, or
> a business meeting with a bad taste in our mouth. How seldom
> have long talks proved to be good and fruitful? Would not
> many if not most of the words we use be better left unspoken?
> We speak about the events of the world, but how often do we
> really change them for the better? We speak about people and
> their ways, but how often do our words do them or us any
> good? We speak about our ideas and feelings as if everyone
> were interested in them, but how often do we really feel under-
> stood? . . . . Words often leave us with a sense of inner defeat.
> (1981, 51–52)

I had read those words, and concurred, at a time in my life
when I felt called to retreat and silence. But, as so often happens, the
practice of any discipline causes its opposite to erupt in our lives
with a compelling demand for attention. There I was, ready to retire
under my card table with the conch-shell light, but instead I found
myself summoned to a conversation that has gone on since 1986.

In order to practice radical presence—to come home to
your heart and listen deeply to others who look for you there—
someone must first listen to *you*. Celtic spirituality calls this person the *Anam Chara*, or soul friend. For years I had wished for a
true spiritual teacher, and meditated on the Buddhist saying,
"When the student is ready, the teacher will arrive." I never
seemed to be ready—although I suspect I am the kind of person
who never will be ready because I am congenitally suspicious of
gurus. What I found instead was a buddy: a relationship that may
incarnate the Northern Minnesota summer camp version of soul
friend. His name is Peter Crysdale, a Quaker minister and social
activist, and at the time he was looking for a buddy as well.

16

As Peter and I became friends, we decided to spend two hours a week in a process we called "deep listening." Both of us felt a need for spiritual direction, but neither of us knew any Jesuits. We developed a simple formula: you talk for an hour, and then I talk for an hour. We didn't plan to ask a lot of questions, or interrupt much beyond a few clarifications, or give advice. At various times, we broke most of those rules. We moved five hundred miles away from each other. But the conversations (by phone now) have continued for more than a decade. In this trusty concord, I am beginning to learn to listen; I am beginning to be able to stand being heard. It's frightening because true attention, like Rilke's Apollo, invites us to change.

How does this listening work and what's deep about it? Don't all of us know how to listen? On the contrary, I think we know how to shut down. Self-preservation compels it. Modern life—with its din of Muzak and commercial entreaty, its appeals and drives, its reviews and performance evaluations—trains us not to attend but to tune out. There is much to hear, but little worth listening to. In an environment of overstimulation, the commitment to spend time, simply listening, constitutes a radical experiment in friendship. I know a woman who has raised twelve foster children. She uses a wheelchair, and is in fact paralyzed from the neck down, but she cares for children with attention and presence. "I am always here," she says, "and I listen." Listens, I would venture, *deeply*. Attention and presence imply something more like Zen meditation or centering prayer than like the "communication skills" we go to workshops to master. When I am present—to meditation, to art, to another—the feeling I have, incommunicable as it may be, comes to me as a sort of cello continuum under the buzz of life. Peter and I talk and laugh and badger each other, but under it all runs this cello note of *presence*, and that's what makes the thing work.

The *you-talk-then-I-talk* rule is the one we most often keep. It's essential to our dynamic, because Peter tends to dominate conversations, and I tend to drop the conversational ball and start staring at leaf hoppers and shifts of light. But we have tried and discarded most other contemporary guidelines for spiritual direction. In a certain sense, we are old-fashioned. We often scold each other and give orders, like medieval monastics. This is not supposed to happen in the therapeutic model many people apply to spiritual direction today. But spiritual direction is nothing much like psychotherapy. For me, it is like talking to a prophet in the wilderness. (I think Peter probably eats locusts. I often hear something crunching on the phone, but he tells me they are corn chips.)

We are both solitary, short-tempered people, and we don't have the patience for a lot of psychological soft shoe. My notes on conversations with

Peter are full of his patriarchal commands, ranging from "Stop resisting and pay attention to what you're supposed to be doing with your life" to "Get your mechanic to reset the idle on the Toyota." For my part, I once wrote up a "Holy Rule" for Peter and told him to tape it to his wall. It was full of matriarchal counsel, like "Don't eat standing up. Don't fall asleep in your clothes."

"My friend Judy is always whining," I tell him. "So are you," he says back. "What are you doing now? Whining about your friend Judy."

I apologize. "I'm sorry, I'm whining."

"That's what friends are for. To whine and whine and whine to. Don't ever stop whining. It's a spiritual practice."

The bluntness of our conversations comes of long listening and deep trust, in particular a trust that neither has a vested interest in changing the other, nor has a cultural or religious paradigm to impose. We have suffered and forgiven each other through deep and painful misunderstandings: indeed, Peter has helped me to learn that intimacy entails pain, almost as a condition of growth. This history has given us the capacity to renegotiate definitions of being male, female, ministers, teachers, spiritual beings, social beings—and so on—within the frameworks of our eccentric temperaments.

Peter, for example, is quarrelsome and disorganized. A traditional guidance might try to "break" him of those habits, but why? Being present to Peter's contentiousness has helped me to understand a lot about male, as opposed to female, spirituality and to remember that both the lion and the lamb are permitted to lie down in the peaceable kingdom. Many of our models for being spiritual people are feminized models. And when men get into spiritual relationships with women—I'm thinking of the conversations of Francis and Clare of Assisi, Teresa of Avila and John of the Cross, Frances de Sales and Jane de Chantal—they tend to appropriate feminine language.

We should celebrate this, I'm sure: the ceremonies of innocence in a violent world. Only I, for my part, am not very meek, nor is my dear companion. Anyone who thinks spiritual direction is for monks and hermits—people called to "states of perfection" in the old spiritual hierarchy—can take a tour around Peter and me to get a more realistic vision. Perfection is not on our horizon: we are *not* very good or very successful; we are *not* Francis and Clare. Both of us, for example, are divorced, crochety, and often on the outs with our communities. We screw up relationships; we are not team players. We participate in the reality of brokenness that many spiritual people affirm abstractly but avoid by grace, luck, or a preference for safety. Spiritual people, by and large, try to behave well, a habit that I am not attempting to subvert. Still, living by some idea about how things should be is not entirely preferable to living as who you are. For one thing, the goodness of others can have a shaming side, especially if the virtue has shallow roots. People who do not or cannot, yet, behave very well may feel humiliated by spiritual language and behavior. They may feel they aren't good enough to sit at this table. Or they may suspect, with reason, the quality of the food.

In a relationship of deep listening, Peter and I have given each other freedom to chart a spiritual path outside the norm, which has helped us to see what the norms are and what they are good for, and where they may actually impede spiritual progress. I mentioned Peter's disorganization. In Myers-Briggs' terms, he's a strong "P." In the orderly parochial halls of my childhood religion, spiritual direction seemed to assume that "P"s are bad spiritual material, who should be fixed or cured. Our deeply puritan traditions, maybe, have taught us to affirm the steady, solid, frugal, orderly religious model. Dealing with Peter has helped me—me with the color-coded file drawers—to understand the beauty of a spirit that is truly on call. If Peter is late, it's because whoever he is with at the moment has his full attention. Many's the time I have watched him wend his way toward a meeting with some important official, or donor, or me and—deflected by some grandmother or wandering felon—stop to talk, stop to listen. Once I gave him, with wistful hope, a Mickey Mouse watch. He soon lost it.

Attention: deep listening. People are dying in spirit for lack of it. In academic culture most listening is critical listening. We tend to pay attention only long enough to develop a counterargument; we critique the student's or the colleague's ideas; we mentally grade and pigeonhole each other. In society at large, people often listen with an agenda, to sell or petition or seduce. Seldom is there a deep, openhearted, unjudging reception of the other. And so we all talk louder and more stridently and with a terrible desperation. By contrast, if someone truly listens to me, my spirit begins to expand.

I once spent the summer with a mixed bag of American and British students at an English university. One of our lecturers was a famous British academic, very fierce and unapproachable. But because we American students were unfamiliar with the British style, we found him funny and laughed uproariously at his twitty comments on Queen Victoria. The more we Americans laughed, the better and the wittier grew his lectures. The decorous British students shook their heads in disbelief over the transformation of their famous scholar into the Monty Python of Exeter College. In our welcoming (though perhaps befuddled) response, we mirrored back to him a self he had not known before. Still, it was a self longing to be born and perform for the pleasure of all. So it is with spiritual companionship. If someone pays attention to the part of me that struggles for transcendence, my search intensifies, the questing spirit grows bold enough to claim its path. I live more thoroughly and bravely in sacred time.

Now, sacred time runs on a daily clock. I want to emphasize again how banal, how unassuming, is this relationship of deep listening. I sit in my kitchen in St. Paul drinking tea, listening to Peter crunch corn chips in Berkeley; we talk about our struggles with child rearing, our jobs, our ex-spouses, our cars, our dates, our pets. By what right do we call this a spiritual friendship? Because of the intention, for one thing. Because of the gift, for another: I've come to understand that certain people do or do not have a gift for loving a certain partner, teaching a particular student, training one dog or another. Peter and I have a gift—hard-won—for this relationship and it's fair to acknowledge that. And, finally, because we know that the junk flowing through our lives is the raw material of new creation. As Brenda Ueland says in her essay about listening, "I think it's only by expressing all that is inside that purer and purer streams come. . . . If you hold back the dull things, you are certain to hold back what is clear and beautiful and true and lively" (1992, 104). This week I may tell Peter how my bad dog, Shep, got up on the kitchen table and ate the butter. Next week, Peter may remind me how similar my spiritual path is to Shep's.

From time to time, I give up on Peter as a spiritual director and consult with a "real" director, priest or nun. I want someone who will give me advice, who knows about psychology and the pratfalls of contemplative prayer. I cherish these encounters, but in them I must struggle not to compartmentalize my life into sacred and secular divisions. The image of perfection intimidates. Perhaps some degree of tension is inevitable when your director lives under vows of poverty and chastity while you struggle with kids' financial aid forms and importunate boyfriends. I have even known people in spiritual direction to be positively duplicitous with their directors, to construct one self, as it were, for the hermitage and another for daily life.

Listening in the kitchen, this evasion is not so easy. Peter and I certainly do resist and hide out from each other, just as we resist our deepest sense of call. Sometimes we even hang up the phone. Other times, though, we ring up in the middle of the night. Our angels are, like Rilke's, earth angels, who often fly in the dark. They specialize in the panic surrounding sick children, creepy noises in the basement, and teenagers who have missed curfew. I suppose we could mull over these things without calling each other; sometimes we have to go it alone. But why did Jesus send the apostles out in pairs, besides to share corn chips?

I practiced Zen meditation for thirty years before I began to understand how its attitude of reflection could be transferred to everyday life.

Similarly, I practiced the discipline of deep listening for a long time before I realized that it, too, was a branch of contemplation. Like all contemplative disciplines, it deals with the whole rather than with the parts: it attends not to the momentary faltering but to the long path of the soul, not to the stammer, but to the poem being born. It completes the clumsy gesture in an arc of grace. One can, I think, *listen someone into existence*, encourage a stronger self to emerge or a new talent to flourish. Good teachers listen this way, as do terrific grandfathers and similar heroes of the spirit. The critical hearer, by contrast, crushes our spirits, leaves us with that sense of inner defeat Henri Nouwen speaks of.

Brenda Ueland understood well this contemplative dimension of listening. "In order to learn to listen," she tells us,

> here are some suggestions: Try to learn tranquility, to live in the present a part of the time every day. Sometimes say to yourself: "Now. What is happening now? This friend is talking. I am quiet. There is endless time. I hear it, every word." Then, suddenly, you begin to hear not only what people are saying, but what they are trying to say, and you sense the whole truth about them. And you sense existence, not piecemeal, not this object and that, but as a translucent whole. (1992, 109)

4

Listening Like a Cow

SEVERAL YEARS AGO I BEGAN TO THINK ABOUT WHAT IT WOULD mean to try to locate our work as teachers within the spiritual traditions of humankind—to relocate it, I should say, because education in all cultures has radiated from monasteries, ashrams, and yeshivas: from spiritual sites that represent the deepest longings of human community. Perhaps because of my long conversation with Peter, I was particularly aware that all of these traditions constellate around the ancient model of spiritual direction as a way of understanding what goes on between teacher and student. The conventions of spiritual direction structure the interaction between a seeker and the mentor he or she chooses to follow.

If you want to learn, it makes sense to seek help from one who has already taken the path. In the fourth century, for example, spiritual people fleeing much the same market pressures as we face today emigrated into the desert to find solitude. No sooner had they settled into their huts when a crowd of followers appeared looking for advice about how to live alone. These early monastics, who became known as the desert fathers and mothers, began one of the earliest traditions of spiritual direction. In Russia, similarly, until this century, each village tended to have its *staretz*, or hermit, who communed with God for the good of all. The *startzi*, too, kept open house for those seeking advice and counsel. Even such medieval anchorites as Julian of Norwich, who walled herself up in the parish church, received a daily stream of villagers at her little window. In modern times, monks and nuns have functioned as spiritual directors for lay people who seek help on the spiritual path; there are similar lineages of direction in Buddhism, Judaism, and every other spiritual tradition I know of.

Perhaps it's daunting to imagine our work in such a context. Realistic humility moves me to substitute a more egalitarian notion, such as "companioning," for the directive language of the tradition. Even at that, some fundamental distinctions must be made. When I experiment with spiritual direction as a model for teaching, I'm using the concept in a general and metaphoric sense. Some religious traditions encourage the teacher (or the shop steward, physician, or assembly line worker) to intervene in the religious quest of coworkers and fellow travellers whenever possible, to seek out opportunities for evangelizing. This is not my intention, and evangelization does not enter into my goals.

Still, I must return to a point I've been making all along: whether we are aware of it or not, professional life tends to be dominated by one or another set of metaphors. We have to be conscious about the metaphors we choose to describe our relationship to students, and resist those thrust upon us by the marketplace. Will you slide into the role of friendly shopkeeper, or will you choose to situate yourself in a tradition that calls the best in you and your students to account?

Spiritual companioning implies deep and intentional listening, but it can and probably should be an unpretentious relationship. It needn't grant authority to one or the other listening partner, but, like my chats with Peter, it can fruitfully go back and forth. It may begin in friendship or mentoring or—as one of my most cherished companionships did—in daily sharing of physical work.

Permit me to shift the scene here away from the English department to a job I had a few years ago as (so my passport read) an agricultural laborer. I was working in a cattle barn and at the same time I was formally studying spiritual direction in an academic program; occasionally, I would take off on the passport in question to immerse myself in the life of a Buddhist monastery across the world. In teaching, it would be hard to merge such disparate lives (what does that tell us?) but in farming the threads twisted easily around each other. Barns are great contemplative spaces, and workers feeding and caring for animals fall into a kind of Benedictine rhythm together. My best friend and spiritual companion in those days was a young farmer named Dan.

One day, while we were pitching corn into the bunks of fifty black-faced Suffolk ewes, Dan started to tell me about "advances" in his professional world. With pride he went on about dairy barns that operate twenty-four hours a day, huge operations where the cows are moved around on conveyor belts. Farmers, like teachers, sometimes doubt their worth in the modern economy, and I could hear in Dan's voice the rising note of desperation that overtakes a person trying to convince himself that his chosen work is valued by those in power. As he explained it all, he shifted restlessly from boot to boot and nervously bent the rim of his feed cap. I sensed a current of loathing that ran along beside his fascination with technical advance. I butted in with a version of my favorite question, "Who are you and what are you doing here?" I put it this way: "Is that how you want to run your barn?"

"No!" It was a cry from the heart, so vehement that I had to step back a few paces and sit down on a bale of alfalfa hay. "But Mary," he went on, "I have to, I have to compete." Farmers, too, get lost in the mall.

"Dan, this is your *life*. How you run your barn has to be connected to who you *are*."

As I listened to him, I could feel his spirit lighten. Freed for the moment from despair and robo-cows, he began to talk about other alternatives: community farming, sustainable agriculture, niche marketing. These were radical ideas in the small world where our conversation was taking place. Hanging around the co-op with other farmers committed to factory farming, he wouldn't have had the freedom to discuss these alternatives. But because somebody sat down and listened to the deep subterranean stream of his identity, he began to have dreams, see visions.

Presence to another can be this informal and this life-saving. You don't need any more office than a bale of hay. But you do need to pay attention to another at the place where his or her soul is on the line. And, in my experience, the gift goes back and forth. As often as I was Dan's teacher, he was mine. I was his novice. Skulking around the barn in my filthy snowmobile suit, I gave new meaning to the word. Dan, with his own kindly attention, made claims on my identity that I'm still trying to answer.

With this homely example, I hope to democratize the idea of spiritual direction. I can't place myself, without laughing out loud, in line with the desert *ammas*; the choices of my life have led me deep into the world rather than to a position of spiritual authority. But anybody can sit on a bale of hay and pay attention.

We learn to listen by being listened to: by our parents, if we are lucky; by a therapist, perhaps; by friends; and, as I've suggested, in a formal or informal relationship of spiritual direction. And once we've been listened to and continue to be listened to by loving presence, we can pass on the gift.

Jim Farrell, a colleague of mine at St. Olaf College in Northfield, Minnesota, recently invited me into a series of discussions the faculty were having around the topic of "healing stories." I immediately became captivated by the phrase, which seems to have direct relevance to the work we do as teachers of writing and literature. Stories started to rise like trout. Stories that healed, stories that saved lives. Recently I saw a sculpture from the Hopi culture that portrays a woman with an inward look and an open mouth holding on each knee a listening child. Sometimes I am that woman.

Sometimes we are all called to be that woman. Sometimes I am that listening child. These roles, buried in us, sleeping in us, I would suggest, are as important as other roles we play in professional life. Between the storyteller and the listening child we can construct a ground of sanity amidst the dislocations of our days.

Stories that rise: this one was told to me by a friend who, like many of us, has a piece of music that she thinks of as "her song," music you play in your mind or on your cassette deck when things are going very badly or very well. Her song is the boy-soprano duet in the "Agnus Dei" from Andrew Lloyd Weber's *Requiem.*

My friend was going through a terrible time in her life—I'll skip the details, because it's her story. On one of the worst days, as many of us might do at such a time, she drove to someplace like the Mall of America. But it was such a bad day that once she got there she just collapsed on the front seat of her Volvo.

She was sitting there in a state of heartbreak when suddenly she heard a pure boy soprano singing "Agnus Dei . . . Agnus Dei . . ."

She snapped to attention. She thought she was hallucinating. She looked around. Nothing. It was the middle of summer, and she was parked near a bus kiosk. She looked in the window of the kiosk and saw up against the window the soles of size twelve tennis shoes. She saw a baseball fly up and descend, fly up and descend. She heard the recurrent plop of the ball in the leather mitt, and the pure boy voice singing "Agnus Dei . . . Agnus Dei."

I don't have a philosophical position on what is or is not a healing story, but this one has the earmarks. This is a story I know my friend will tell to her grandchildren, one on each knee, with her mouth open and an inward look on her face. A story that says the universe knows our song.

Those of us who are teachers of English, I sometimes tell myself, are in the discipline of storytelling. We are like old shamans sitting around the fire scaring people half to death, or saving their lives, or healing their hearts. (Historians do this as well, but they do not readily admit it.) I teach literature and writing, so in my classes it is a two-way street: I tell stories and I listen to stories. It's quite a weird job for a grown-up.

If one is aware of storytelling as a way of being present in the world, one soon becomes aware of its opposite: not telling. If we can't tell our story, if it's caught in our throat, it seems to block our spirit's longing to participate in the world. At an extreme, we can't reach out at all. And everybody, I think, has a story or two caught in the throat.

I had a student some years ago who couldn't do his writing assignments. He wasn't much of a talker, either. He sat in misery day after day, completely inarticulate no matter how anyone tried to intervene. We had cajoled the writing block with free-writing, we had written it polite letters of inquiry. Finally we had to rest in contemplation of its vast, solid will.

Then one day the young man came to my office. In the course of two hours, he managed to get out about five sentences. He told me that his mother had died suddenly a few years before, and since then his father had become completely mute. This silence spread out in the family. No one was allowed to say anything at the dinner table, not even "pass the salt."

Our two-hour session did not seem to change anything. The student never did complete an assignment and finally dropped the course. But a couple of years later he came to see me and to bring me a present, a book by Henri Nouwen called *The Genesee Diary*. I didn't read it for several years because at that time in my life I was suspicious of anything religious and Nouwen was a Catholic priest.

The young man said, "You know that day I came to see you? I was on my way to kill myself." Then we had a cup of tea and he went about his business. There was no drama: just "I'm alive. Here's a book you may like. See you." And I want to emphasize the quiet, inward character of this story because I think that if we are ever—just now and then—paying attention, we save each other's lives and sanity with quiet, natural gestures unobserved even by ourselves. Life is a great search-and-rescue mission, stranger than the novels of Charles Williams.

There's more to this story. When I finally got around to reading *The Genesee Diary*, it was at a stage in my own life when I was pretty much in the condition of the friend who folded up in her Volvo. It was the book I needed. It was the book that knew my song.

But our stories are caught in our throats. We need someone to listen to our stuttering, stammering plea to be heard. We need deep listening. We need good, welcoming silence, not the dark, crushing silence of my student's house. When this attentive silence opens to me, I gather the courage to speak, to be heard, to hear myself.

Is it possible to carry this listening silence into our work? What a radical idea: it seems, doesn't it, to be the exact opposite of our job description. When I was working on my Ph.D., the caretaker at my apartment building used to tell me about his own two daughters: "One's a medical doctor, one's a talking doctor."

But what if we did the opposite of what everyone expects of us?

A few years ago I taught a senior seminar called "Rhetoric of Spiritual Autobiography." One of the students, when it was his turn to lead, chose to begin the class with five minutes of silent meditation, then five minutes of writing. That day we were exploring a Jungian analysis of water imagery in the writings of Teresa of Avila. Each student in turn read a little of what he or she had written. Now this is Minnesota, and water imagery is a seductive subject. One young woman had written about going to The Lake, an archetypal Minnesota site. Suddenly she began to cry, because, as it turned out, her family's cabin had burned down that weekend. Finally, she bolted from the room.

Let's examine how many things have gone wrong here, from the point of view of a young seminar leader with his grade on the line, his friends watching, and some spiritual business of his own to pursue. What must he be asking himself? I know the answer to that, because the leader called a break and immediately turned to me. Is it OK to cry in class? Is it OK to leave the room? If that happens, what should the seminar leader do? Was it wrong to begin with silence? Did the silence make something happen, and what should we all do now?

Whenever you move any small peg in classroom culture—or the culture of any organization—everything you used to take for granted will shift. Things get interesting, because people have to wake up and move out of their programmed behavior. In a collaborative class, which a senior seminar certainly ought to be, I have to rely on the collective energy of the group to solve problems as they rise. It's well to remember that there's a great deal more creativity in the room than may reside in the teacher. In this instance, one of the students, who happened to be a nurse, followed the young woman into the restroom and comforted her.

What I had to tell the worried seminar leader was that, so far, he had been leading one of the best class discussions I'd ever heard. He had spoken so gently and quietly, allowed such calm pauses between each exchange, that people felt free to speak from the heart. They sensed they would be *heard*. Being heard might well make *me* cry and bolt.

Having your lake home burn down is not so bad, compared to lots of things people have to tell. It wasn't a story about death or sexual abuse, which also can come up in class. I mention these things because some of my colleagues are worried about how to handle such revelations. In the abstract, I don't know. In the concrete: *pay attention* was my advice to the seminar leader. "How can we go on?" he wanted to know.

"Pay attention," I told him. "Just be there. Don't be thinking about a solution, or how you should fix it. Just listen hard and try to be present." It's very bad business to invite heartfelt speech and then not listen.

Everyone made it back from break, including the woman who had fled, and we went on with our exploration of the interior castle.

For my part, I encourage students to protect their margins of safety and I don't encourage a confessional atmosphere—although other teachers do wonderful work from a completely different perspective. Even so, people sometimes feel led to speak about painful subjects and that may create a crisis for the hearers. Better that crisis than a classroom where nothing is at stake.

But *what to do*? I handle crisis in the classroom in a kind of inarticulate, dumb cow way. I don't recommend this approach; I'll just tell a story about it. A few years ago a man in a workshop I was leading wrote an essay about being seduced by his art teacher. After he read it, I looked at him like a black-and-white heifer and said nothing. This wasn't pedagogy, by the way, this was stupidity. There was silence, then some discussion, I don't remember of what. Later he wrote me a letter in which he said, "When you didn't respond to my seduction story, I was furious. I really wanted a lot of attention for that. Then I felt a great lightening of my soul. I was *free* of that story. It fell into that space of silence and just blew away. I could go on and stop obsessing. I started painting again."

That was a good result, I guess, but of course it might just as well have been a bad result. It could be that people sometimes leave my class feeling I don't care. The fact is, I would not be able to care very long if I thought it was up to me to make a wise comment about everything people tell me, or to fix them. That would be overreaching, all right. Life comes to dark places, and people sit with stories that are truly hellacious. Things happen to all of us that wouldn't happen in a just universe to the most vicious felons. But I often find it impossible to *say* anything about these events. I listen with what love I can muster. I don't put this forward as a theory of response, but rather as a statement about my deficiency. Words are an insult to the pain of much experience, or the complexity of it. And I am a rather silent person by nature or lack of glibness. I say this because I think there are a lot of people like me in Minnesota and elsewhere.

What does this have to do with teaching school, you may wonder. Well, I think that if we can't pull the weight of these stories off people, it's very hard for them to learn. Such stories lie on the soul like the hungry ghosts of Buddhist legend. Students, and teachers too, might as well come to class and say, "I'm sorry I can't think. I have a terrible heavy ghost lying on my soul and draining it of all energy." We have to lift the weight before the student can learn anything. Fortunately, moving ghosts is a team effort. The teacher is seldom in it alone. Lots of people are helping that you'll probably never know about, not only the counsellors and chaplains, but the food service workers and office staff. I know two college students who, on every break, go back to their high school to visit the janitor: someone who leaned on her broom and listened.

What I'm trying to construct here is a theory of attention that depends little on therapeutic skills and formal training: listening like a cow. Those of you who grew up in the country know that cows are good listeners. And barns, as I said before, are great contemplative spaces—at least the old ones were. I recommend to you this kind of dairy barn listening. We don't need fixing, most of us, as much as we need a warm space and a good cow. Cows cock their big brown eyes at you and twitch their ears when you talk. This is a great antidote to the critical listening that goes on in academia, where we listen for the mistake, the flaw in the argument. Cows, by contrast, manage at least the appearance of deep, openhearted attention.

If you are listening, if you are turning your big brown or blue eyes on somebody and twitching your ears at them, you are earning your silage. You are listening people into existence. You are saving lives. You are producing Grade A.

5

Looking at the Moon

THE GOAL OF SPIRITUAL DIRECTION IS TO SUPPORT THE transformation of the one seeking direction. By "transformation" I mean movement toward truth, true self, authenticity. Transformation occurs in a kind of spiral. At the outer whirl of the spiral, a lot of analytical activity may occur: the badgering and bossing of certain Mother Superiors and Zen masters, therapy talk, analytical discussion, the passing on of the precepts of a tradition or the practical application of them to daily life. At the innermost point of the spiral, though, is a silence: a place of presence. Transformation happens in the badgering and bothering (and correcting and grading); it happens as well on the ground of silence. Good teaching or counselling—and I am thinking here more of what goes on in individual mentoring than in the classroom—begins in the contemplative presence of both companions, although this inward attention may not enter explicitly into their time together; the session may be devoted to analyzing an essay or sorting out a financial aid crisis. And the teacher may be more ready to center than the student (or vice versa); for our part, it's helpful to signal by our greeting, our office arrangements, and other nonverbal cues, that the seeker has entered upon some kind of holy ground.

I do not mean solemn ground. I say this having once taught a freshman class with a foundling kitten in the pocket of my jumper. On my way to class that morning, a neighbor had asked me if I would try to find a home for the kitten. Feline need, on this occasion, corresponded with a period of midterm doldrums in my freshman class. The kitten's visit brought us all to delighted attention: one of those happenings that disrupts classroom order just enough to wake us up. Paradox, humor, and play pull us out of our stale mental worlds and into the *now*. If we remember that the German word for *holy* (*selig*) is the root of our word *silly*, we may be forced to make some pertinent connections.

A woman I know, formerly a Berkeley anthropology student and now a Buddhist nun, Sister Thanh Minh, told me a story that illustrates how routine mentoring moves into contemplative presence. "Something was troubling me," she said, "and I asked advice of a Buddhist monk who was leading our retreat. He told me to meet him in the garden, under the full moon. We sat down. He looked for a moment at the moon. Then he folded his robes under him and assumed the lotus position. He closed his eyes and said, *'Now I am ready to listen.'* I talked for an hour and then he opened his eyes. He said, *'I understand what you are saying.'"*

Sister Thanh Minh concluded, "When someone listens like that, your life is up for grabs."

I do not habitually receive students in the lotus position nor do I meet them under the full moon. Still, I must allow this story to influence my demeanor when a visitor knocks. The image speaks to my best sense of the task of directing students. We listen with absolute taking-in of the other. We become sacramental, in the sense that we are the outward sign of the other's inner life. No advice may be given, but change occurs because the encounter stirs us at the level of soul, or because we open a window through which transformative energy flows. The teacher allows himself or herself to be used as a kind of lightning rod for the sacred. Or for holy silliness. A joke can be equally unsettling to the quotidian world, can startle us into the present moment and bring us home to our hearts.

What we say, in our encounters, is less important than how present we are able to be. John Woolman, the eighteenth-century Quaker abolitionist, while preaching a sermon in the Native American community of Wayalusing, declined the services of a translator. He felt that too much attention to syntax would interfere with the "tendering of hearts." One of the hearers, a man named Papunehang, responded, "I love to feel where words come from" (1989, 133). If we read Woolman's journals, we cannot help but conclude that he consistently dwelt not in words, arguments, and analysis, but in the place *where words come from.* The encounters he records on his journeys were rather like those of Sister Thanh Minh and her teacher. Woolman never lectured or hectored his auditors on the subject dear to his heart, abolition. He simply listened and people changed. "When you are listened to like that, your life is up for grabs."

Louis Evely makes a similar point about teaching: "The really moving thing in the work of education is listening to a person at the deepest level while preserving round all that he confides us of himself a halo of mystery, patience, care and love, thanks to which, sometimes, we can free him from what he is and give him access to his future" (1970, 78).

Having spoken so strongly on behalf of deep listening, I have to admit that the best guidance in my own life has been characterized more by what I have (affectionately) called "badgering and bothering" than by contemplative presence. My best teachers have all been talkers rather than listeners. And I don't know how I would respond to a teacher who simply listened deeply. I might be struck dumb with shyness. I will come back to this paradox in a moment.

For now, I will simply locate my preference in the exigencies of personality: most of the odd things I do in the classroom have evolved from the struggle all of us go through between the norms of our discipline and the demands of who we are. Many teachers are clever at giving advice; for them, the lectern is a congenial and bully pulpit. For my part, I'm disinclined to be directive about anything more complicated than the construction of a paragraph. Even the conscientious marginal notes I write on student papers often seem a time-consuming exercise in futility for me and for my students. I am particularly aware of this now, having recently spent time being a student again and reading my own teachers' comments with utter incomprehension: what could these hieroglyphics possibly mean?

In recent years, English teachers have tried to get away from the kind of prescriptive commentary that used to be the norm in our discipline (although my recent experience as a student would suggest that authoritarian correction remains very much in vogue elsewhere in academia). We've learned to respond, as friendly readers, to an evolving text—"I need more information here" or "I'm lost!"—rather than bossily telling people what to do. This new etiquette of guidance might be framed within a broader context of listening to students: such commentary respects a person's ability to reenter his or her own life and reconfigure and transform it. Our most productive comments can do no more than hold open a space into which the student may in time grow.

The revision process, in life and art, revolves around a meta-comment we would probably never make: "Go home and grow some more!" One of my own manuscripts has just come back from an editor covered in painstaking editorial suggestions that I know I am not mature enough to follow. I only hope, like a student gnawing her nails at midterm, that I can extend the deadline until my inner life progresses sufficiently to effect a revision.

6

Dissonance

NOW I WANT TO RETURN TO THE PARADOX TOUCHED ON EARLIER: silent attention helps us to grow, but good advice, intervention, and challenge also nudge us out of difficulties and help us to revise the most intractable life or essay.

I think that my own quandary over guiding students reflects a problem that has vexed me in many areas of endeavor. It has to do with moving, often uncomfortably, between the analytical and intuitive aspects of life. As a young mother, I used to feel this dissonance keenly at the change of seasons. In summer, I would sink into "child mind," wandering around to the rhythms of our toddlers. Space and time seemed to expand; the garden went on forever, the picnic's conclusion defined only by darkness falling. Autumn came with its painful dislocation; fifty minutes meant fifty minutes precisely, and a new wave of students would rush in, unforgiving as the tide, if you didn't snap your briefcase and move along. In the midst of this transition, outlining a syllabus always gave me a stomachache. How could one predict and define the likely motion of fifty freshmen up and down the terrain of poetry or the expository essay? Every day's movement between home and school presented a little microcosmic struggle between these colliding worlds: between a mother's open, present mode of being and the analytical demands of my job.

You don't have to be a mother to experience this conflict: being a poet versus being a teacher strains me even more. African American and Hispanic colleagues have given me both comic and heartrending insights into the dissonance between the neighborhood of origin and the professional world. Contending elements in the self, however we may define them—intuitive/analytical, multi-racial, gay/straight, female/male—give us pain, present us with quandaries, expand our consciousness, prevent boredom, and nudge us toward living a more integrated life. Internal

33

division, however painful, forces us to refigure the world. Our inner "diversity issues" challenge our colleagues as well, because they have to deal with us and expand their own definitions of what's real.

What's called "reality" may simply incarnate some dominant cultural myth. Someone who doesn't share the myth is in for periodic jolts. For example, I recently attended a preterm workshop on student counselling in which the facilitators presented as objective data what is in fact a version of the American white male quest story: the job of the freshman student, they told us, is to separate from the family and individuate. Well, yes and no. What if we were to define our job as *nurturing* the student's relationship to family and neighborhood, mediating the differences between university and home life? Might that not avoid some of the alienation students feel, that, indeed, most humans feel as they try to bridge their professional lives and the life that came before that?

In order for any of us as individuals to critique the cultural myths that oppress us—and I include white males in this community of suffering—we are called to an elemental act of mediation. We have to have a few conversations with the pain in our gut; we have to know the world outside and the world within, value both and give both their due. For anyone enduring the pain of dissonance, this is a brave act of integration and a generous contribution to the community. Too often we either submit and surrender our souls to the social consensus, or withdraw in passive narcissism.

My own internal divisions are less painful than those suffered by colleagues I learn from every day: "intuitive" is not exactly a marginalized minority. Still, the struggle between my oceanic instincts and my analytical training defines the way I put together the world. It gives me trouble. Trying to mediate among the clamoring members of my inner committee, I've learned to avoid the word *versus*. But you can't do that with an eraser or a keystroke. Being in poet-mind (receptive, undefended, connected) can make you *prey* in a classroom of sophomores unless you have allowed yourself to be so healed (as one of my teachers said of Francis of Assisi) that you can talk to the birds. Besides, I love the analytical side of my work, its naming of parts. All of us long to create an inner world big enough to comprehend our whole selves.

How are we to do that? A hint of an answer came to me during my recent stay at Thich N'hat Hanh's monastery, Plum Village, in France. I carried with me a question, though I did not know I was carrying it—I had not quite phrased it to myself. But I must have been carrying it, because everything at Plum Village contrived to confront me with answers to it. The question was: How can I honor both the intuitive and analytical aspects of my mind, silencing neither? I have learned now to call that a *koan*. In the Buddhist tradition, a koan is a sort of resonating question that a master gives a student to help that student advance in spiritual understanding or come to enlightenment. In a certain sense, koans are unanswerable; they are intended to lead the student beyond a range of comfortable cognitive strategies.

Koanic understanding demands *presence*, which Thich N'hat Hanh calls simply "washing dishes to wash dishes." Similarly, we could teach simply to teach. If we are well and truly present, no doubt we will say what students need to hear. Every year, no matter how long I have been teaching, I panic the week before Labor Day: I do not remember how to do the job; I have chosen the wrong books; perhaps students have changed and I will not be able to speak their language. My friend Peter always has to talk me down: "They get what they need, they hear what will help them most, now calm down and just *turn up!*"

Everything at Plum Village, especially the spiritual direction, was oriented to mindfulness and to the practical consequence of mindfulness: transformation. Before going there, I assumed that there was more to be learned than "stopping, breathing, and smiling" (Thich N'hat Hanh's formula at its most elemental)—for I had practiced this Buddhist discipline for many years, excluding the smile, which does not come sincerely to the face of a Northern prairie child. Rather, there was excruciating concentration on stopping, breathing, and smiling. Graduate school of Mindfulness.

My spiritual director in the monastery was a German engineer named Karl, a robust man in his sixties, who liked to give advice and gave it with utmost clarity. There was nothing contemplative about our conversations; he was *training* me. In particular, he was schooling me in the management of irritation. Other sojourners were working on grief or depression; I was merely cold, hungry, and mad at my roommates. At Plum Village I often felt like an oyster dumped onto a particularly sandy bank. Everything irritated my tender skin—the food, the cold, the hierarchy, and most of all other people. The advantage of spending a month at a place like Plum Village is that you can hear the dharma in a sort of laboratory environment, constantly thrown back on the difficulties of practicing it. Spiritual direction consisted of practical help in applying the practice to daily annoyances: shrieking attacks from a Vietnamese sister who was convinced I had stolen her gardening shears, vexation of a roommate who wanted the light on all night.

"Valerie really pushes my buttons," I might tell Karl.

"The important thing is to remember that they're *your* buttons. They don't exist out there on some cosmic control panel. Therefore your irritation is based merely on an idea of how things should be. A relative idea. You are producing the feeling from an underlying perception that skews your judgment. You have to get at the underlying idea."

"How do I do that?"

"It's very delicate and intelligent work. You have to wait. When I'm angry, I find at the roots of it some old hurt, some pride, some mistaken idea. That is the important aspect of practice. That is the transforming element."

Problems, for the Mahayana Buddhist, are not in the phenomenal world but in our minds. Our mental constructions determine whether we are happy or sad or angry. "It is just an *idea* that something should be this way or that way," Karl told me again and again. Even the idea of order, or my favorite, the idea of justice, especially justice to me. (Lights out!)

I did not loosen my hold on these "notions" without struggle.

"Some ideas are the foundation of civilization. Some are bad, some are good," I would tell Karl. Since he is German, I did not bring up the case of Hitler, but no doubt he has heard the name.

"True," said Karl, "but if the goal is to change society, as Thich N'hat Hanh worked hard to do in the Vietnam war days, we do not have to get angry to do it. In fact, anger makes us less productive."

This was a new thought for me, a quiet person who sometimes needs a shock of adrenaline to propel me out of serene rumination. Yet I know that when I get angry other people harden in their positions; anger tends to prolong debate, promote walkouts and foment counterrevolution—all of which steal time from the main agenda. Karl gave me a provocative image of his gentle art of social change: "You observe that something is wrong and you calmly put it right. It is as though you peer at a flower arrangement and reach out to adjust a branch." Karl smiled and leaned across the low table between our zafus to touch an imaginary flower. "With no more emotion than *that.*"

"You can guarantee nothing," Thich N'hat Hanh said in his next dharma talk. "Only dwelling in the present can make us free. We have to look into our suffering, our craving. And when we see its face we will smile: *you cannot make me your prisoner any more.* We have to ask our companions and our teachers to cast light on our aggravation. Peace is every step."

Because we ask our teachers to cast light on our aggravation, there is no such thing as nondirective counselling in the Buddhist tradition. There is no confusion about how one should behave sexually, what constitutes a good diet, etc. At the same time, there is no judgment made about failure. The community is guided by a body of "Precepts," similar to the Judeo-Christian Commandments, but they are best understood as "suggestions" or "pillars of wisdom." It's understood that we will fall short of them. Punishment comes not from God or the teacher but from reality. If you steal or covet you will disturb your peace.

But one's trust in the teacher arises from sharing in the daily, disciplined practice of mindfulness. Morning and evening my teacher, Karl, sat beside me in the zendo: "Upright!" he would crow. "Like a human being!"

One day Thich N'hat Hanh talked about koans. I was not listening very well because I was (as usual) irritated and in pain from sitting upright like a human being on my zafu in the freezing zendo with only a few vegetables in my tummy. Besides, koans are not a major part of the Mahayana tradition, so I had let my mind wander. We have enough koans in daily life: that is the usual Plum Village approach to the subject. But on this occasion Thich N'hat Hanh was filling in the young monks and nuns on some highlights of Rinzai Zen. "You cannot break a koan with your mind," I heard him say. "Mind is like a train on rails; it has to go in a certain direction. Koans remove the rails. Most work of consciousness happens in an underground storehouse that mind can only fertilize like a good gardener. It is not the object of dharma discussion, but of burying, watering, caring for. We trip on a stone and suddenly we understand . . ."

This aside, tossed off and barely listened to, gave me (later, when I tripped on a stone) considerable insight into the balance of *being and doing* in both personal and professional life. Many issues arise: but suppose we were to call them *koans*? You have to make a responsible decision about your best friend's promotion; a sophomore has plagiarized her essay; the grievance committee calls you to hear a sexual harassment concern. Each student, each advisee, each colleague seems to have, at the center of his or her life, a koan of some sort, as I do, in my own inner travail. In the past, I think I've tried to break these problems with my mind, and the result has been sleepless nights, anguished committee meetings, and feelings of emptiness.

How, by contrast, to remove the rails? To let the mystery be mystery and yet to nudge it toward elucidation? Professional life does not allow us to be forever in process: committees meet, semesters end, sexual harassers damage the nets of trust that sustain us. As I review Thich N'hat Hanh's insight into the nature of koan, I believe he is saying, "Mind *alone* has not sufficient power to address the issues of life, yet mind has *some* strength." It's reasonable to fuss over something, and for me this always means a loss of sleep. And I have to prepare and photocopy, annotate, research, and color code.

But, at the same time as I am working out a conscientious analysis, I must honor the soul space of infinite potential. I must drop a query into that underground storehouse and let it grow toward the light in its own time. We have to work with our analytical minds, that is our nature, but we must not trust in mind alone to do the work. There is a ground of knowing below the rattle of cognitive thought. At the deepest level, we have no idea what's going on, why the university is as it is, or why our colleagues and students do the things they do. In the depths of consciousness, these issues are attached to hundreds of thousands of strings. Personal pain is connected to ancient insult; the wounds of history—racism, war, homophobia, cruelty of all kinds—fester unhealed.

The part of me that's an activist does not want to hear this; it impedes my power to get things done. If I act only as an analytical problem solver, however, I make bad decisions, sometimes disastrous decisions. Professional life forces issues to quick resolution, and I must cede to this pressure much of the time, but it is essential to protect an area of inner listening where I remember that the real solutions are in some sense *pending*. Learning to hold the deep issues of life in constant suspension is not a happy process for us poor banished children of Aristotle. Is nothing ever fixed? Probably not. Probably not, but we can *attend* to them; we can be alert. Thomas Merton says somewhere that the issues of life are not problems to be solved but mysteries to be entered.

And even when you are forced to move quickly, try to resist thinking too much. Feel it out, as well. How should I do this in the enclosed spaces of professional life?

"I'm going to work on this all day tomorrow," might productively mean, "I'm going to swim fifteen laps in the pool," or "I am going down to the basement to throw pots." Koans resolve themselves by an internal process, and they are brought to light not by watching but by *not* watching. "I'm going to do this over the weekend" may mean, for me, "I'm going to a hermitage I know of in the woods to pay careful attention to the difference between how oak and aspen leaves stir in the wind."

Gestures like this seem to waste time, but in fact they make more time available to you. I don't know why this is. Perhaps it's a koan.

7

Nourishing the Prophetic Vision

SEVERAL YEARS AGO I WROTE AN ESSAY TITLED "CONFORM, GO Crazy, or Become an Artist." I was keen about this subject because it touches the work closest to my heart, encouraging teachers about the worthiness of the work we do, the necessity of reawakening, if it should be sleeping, our definition of ourselves as artists and visionaries, a call that (in however humble a form) must underlie our decision to become teachers.

I still believe in the prophetic vocation of the teacher, but these days I'm a little more weary, and a diet of honey and locusts falls short of my minimum daily requirements. It occurs to me that exhorting my fellow teachers to take risks every day, to head for the artistic edge, might be enough to do us all in. Prepare your classes; teach school; read student papers; make helpful comments on them; keep office hours; meet with committees; spend quality time with your friends, children, and partners; cut your fat intake; practice meditation; get in your aerobic exercise; and, oh, in your spare time, be a visionary . . .

So I decided to think through a different series of thoughts, beginning with this question: What are the conditions that might make it possible for us to operate at a modest level of prophetic inspiration, to bring a daily beauty to our lives, sustaining to ourselves, our students, and our communities? When I wrote "Conform, Go Crazy, or Become an Artist," I ranted against materialism and the culture of criticism as the enemies of art. It was quite a cosmic analysis. Right now, I'd like to be a little more personal. For the last few months I've been burrowing into my own experience and asking myself what I have learned about creating the conditions necessary to be an artist of whatever kind, of whatever definition: an artist of friendship, of gardening, of making dinner, of making poems—whatever your gift might be. I don't want to preach, to say, "This is what you have to do." I'm just going to say, "Here are some things that worked for me and maybe they'll speak to someone else's condition."

Let me try, first, to establish a frame for thinking about this business of being an artist. I mean it in a very communal and inclusive way. I collect folk art, especially the subclassification called "visionary" art. I started my collection years ago when I taught crafts in a psychiatric hospital. The artwork people made and gave me was strange and beautiful. It *had* to be made. I like art that has a feeling of "I had to make this or die. I had to make this so badly that it didn't bother me that I don't know color theory." So my first question of you, if you wish to begin this inquiry, is "What do you *have to* make? What can only you make?"

Of course I am speaking of visual art in a metaphoric sense. You don't have to start painting on velvet. I am not going to pronounce that overworked word *creativity. Creativity* has for me overtones of superficial activity: frosting on the cake of life. What I'm hoping for is something deeper than that. How can we find our prophetic vision? How can we do what only we are called to do? Bharati Mukherjee, in her book *Jasmine* (1989), talks about how in the Hindu tradition, we might come to earth merely to perform a single minor action essential to the great tapestry of creation: to raise a window or draw back a blind, "to move a flowerpot from one table to another" (53). "The incentive," Jasmine says, "is to treat every second of your existence as a possible assignment from God" (53–54). But what if we miss the moment? What if we are grading papers when we are needed by all the forces of humankind to move a flowerpot? How, given the noise of our lives, can we listen to our deepest call?

Some years ago I spent a sabbatical in a contemplative Quaker community that pretty much unfitted me for the academic world I had left behind. When I came back to my university, I was as confused and befuddled as some kind of alien from a neighboring galaxy. In the year after my sabbatical, I would stare at a photo from the science museum called "Pink Nebula in Orion," a splatter of rosy light, and long for home like E.T.

The problem was, nothing I had learned on sabbatical had fitted me to sit at a desk. In fact, *I* had not come back from sabbatical. Somebody had come back, but it was not the person who left. Still, I had hundreds of things to do, inherited from the person I used to be and no longer was. Teach school, for example. That person had a contract.

I tried very hard to do the work left behind for me by this woman who had gone away and not come back, but the harder I tried, the more I became physically or metaphysically ill. That woman, the former inhabitant of my body, lectured four days a week, three hours a day, just like her colleagues up and down the hall. When I opened my mouth to deliver her lectures, my chest started to hurt and a smothering sensation came over me. I ran out of breath and got faint. It had nothing to do with "getting used to it again," as my helpful colleagues suggested. I just didn't believe the words I was expected to deliver, and my vocal apparatus refused to make the sounds.

I was no longer able to tell my students what they needed to know, because I didn't know what they needed to know, though only a year ago, I had been quite sure.

What are you doing? What are you *really* doing? What is your deepest sense of call? Your true vocation? My "consultant" (something like a spiritual director) in the contemplative community had asked me those questions week after week, and I had come to a vague answer. *To listen,* whatever that might mean. To find out what it might mean. On reentry to this galaxy, I quickly became aware of what it did *not* mean: lecturing on Joseph Conrad, shmoozing at academic cocktail parties. These activities and a few others (some of which were contractual obligations) brought on symptoms that felt like a heart attack. Heart break, maybe. It's easy for me to resist my deepest sense of call, especially if the call interferes with my ambitions about making a living and gaining prestige. But you can't teach school if your lungs won't work. I was confused about priorities, about what I was supposed to be doing. I couldn't possibly get through all the work delegated to the woman whose contract bore my alias, and I was going home every day feeling that, no matter what I had accomplished, I had not done the right thing.

Somewhere in the middle of this crisis, the idea of composing a job description for myself occurred to me. I decided to write down a sentence that reflected my clearest sense of the task. Then I could feel that, whatever else got screwed up, I had been faithful to some inner light. *Peaceful listening,* I wrote on a three-by-five-inch card, and tacked it over my desk. The phrase helped me to pull my days together. When all the phones were ringing, committees meeting, students lining up, I could tell myself, "The only thing that needs to happen is peaceful listening." This turned out to be a useful role for me. Since not too many people were listening to anybody, ever, around the university, I could take up a little slack.

Lecturing, and even the form of pseudo-lecturing called "leading discussion," yielded place to peaceful listening. I began to ask students what they wanted to know. They were willing to tell me. I—the energetic pacer—began to sit down in the classroom, talking to small groups, sometimes talking to one or two students, sending others off to pursue this or that and report back. Gradually I learned to breathe again. Things still piled up on my desk like one of those Welsh mine tips that occasionally slides down and buries a village. But I felt I was doing my job.

I have read that, in a time of crisis, the old myths tell us to *loosen our strings*. "When a woman has reached that dark moon land of No-Return," writes the Jungian analyst Nor Hall, "this would be the time for her to undo every knot on her garments, unlock the doors, open windows, uncork bottles, untie shoelaces, unbraid her hair, set the cows out of their stall, free the chickens, free anything that is tied!"(1980, 102).

Had I not followed some instinctive wisdom, let my academic chickens roam, I would have missed rich lessons. I learned a great deal that year about the dialectics of speech and silence, doing and being. Of course, I've blown most of it, as I inevitably do. I've decided, once again, that I know what my students need, I'm ranting away about my latest theories. I have stopped yearning after strange galaxies. I hardly ever listen to anybody.

But in a few years I will have another sabbatical.

At about the time I returned from the Galaxy Far Away, one of my students died. This happens from time to time. A student dies, a teacher dies. Often we don't think about it much. Where I teach, a professor died a few years ago and most people didn't get to the funeral. We had a very important committee meeting. But when this student, Eileen, died, she helped me to think about it because she shared a lot of her dying with me. She was a middle-aged student—my age, that is—who was being sent to the university by the company she worked for as a condition of being promoted. To the company's surprise, the college required her to take English as well as finance and accounting.

When she was diagnosed with an incurably advanced lung cancer, she told me, her main response had been to read her English texts over and over. Marketing and finance became less relevant. I was happy that she found John Cheever and Virginia Woolf important; but, for my part, I had to ask myself whether Eileen had gotten, in English class, anything she needed to face the fundamental questions of her existence. How had my choice of texts helped? How about my assignments? That year I spent chatting with Eileen about her impending death made me think about what kind of writing I was asking students to do. We think a lot about preparing students for the next level, for their major field courses, for graduate school, for the job. Do we prepare them for *today*?

In Minnesota, in the spring, I often think of the mayfly, who only lives one day. It had better be the right day. In the long sweep of things, I am a mayfly and so are you.

I have a poster of Pablo Cassals on my office door, the great cellist who in mayfly terms lived to be very old. The poster has a quotation that reads, "Resist doing things that have no meaning for life." This is scary advice, advice that can give you a difficult and interesting life. You could wind up on the street, and, as for me, I hope that if I wind up there I have a few musical friends with me and the collected poems of W. B. Yeats.

After you figure out your job description, publish it to your department chair. He or she will probably jump for joy.

Maybe not. In an ideal world, we might define the administrator's task in terms of discerning each individual's gifts and guiding them toward the work most beneficial to self and community. How happy, in this world, your department chair would be to know who you really are (and, for my part, I have been fortunate in working under such a benevolent administration). Instead, so often we hitch race horses to pull wagons, or make those big Clydesdales run races and so on. But let's put aside the judgments of other people: *your* deepest business is to know what kind of horse you are. It took me years and years of concentrated attention to even begin to figure that out.

My next suggestion: keep a Sabbath. My youngest daughter works in the office of a local Hasidic Jewish food service, so we are always wrapped around in Jewish festivals and holidays. It seems that there is always a celebration ready to erupt, or a meaning to be affirmed and witnessed. My daughter was raised in the Quaker tradition; we have a testimony that all days are equal and all to be celebrated—which means that in practice nothing gets celebrated much. But she loves the Hasidic Sabbath. On Friday the excitement starts, with the rabbi—who runs her company—blessing all the workers. On Saturday nobody works and we see the rabbi on his front porch with his prayer shawl on, looking very different than he does on weekdays. We prairie Quakers looked at this for a while and decided there must be something in it.

A couple of months ago I talked to my friend Emily, who is an Episcopalian. She told me that she takes a Sabbath every Monday. "What do you mean?" I said. "What do you do on that day?"

She said, "I just get up on Monday and spend the whole day without a plan. I eat breakfast in or out, or skip breakfast, I call the first person I think of calling. I write a letter if it occurs to me. I drive to Iowa and sit in a cornfield. Whatever. All day. Every Monday."

What is the point of making one day so different from the others? Obviously, this is not the place to reflect theologically, but neither do I want to take a sacred tradition and put it to a merely secular use. I will simply say that it's impossible to hear a subtle call if you do not create a conscious time to listen to it. Who are you and what are you doing here? How do we even *begin* to answer this question? With our heads? With our hearts? One of my friends recently told me that he used to figure things out with his head, but that led to overly intellectual decisions. Then he tried his heart, but that led to overly emotional decisions. "Now," he told me, "I reason with my feet. I look at where I've been walking. Where I tend to turn up. I figure that this might be where I'm going."

With her Monday Sabbath, Emily is, over a period of time, gently watching her feet. After awhile, this may tell her important things about who she is and what she is doing: how she feels without breakfast, who it is important to keep in touch with, what kind of landscape nurtures her spiritually. She is training her intuition.

When I am in my analytical mode, if someone tells me to follow my instincts they might as well tell me to follow a scent like my dog, Shep. If my hind brain ever knew how to do this, it has forgotten. But I think that Emily is following a syllabus for intuition. When you simply follow your feet around for twenty-four hours, you become sensitive to the tiny nudges of spirit.

"I have a feeling I'm wrong about my thesis," one of my students told me in the course of a writing conference.

"What does that feeling feel like?" I asked, really needing to know.

"Like a little mouse tooth, gnawing away," the student replied.

I think we have to give some space and time to learning to see and feel the subtleties of the world around us. Or maybe they are not even subtle, these instincts, intuitions, and visions we shut out. When I take an afternoon of retreat, or even an hour staring at nothing, it's as though a parallel universe comes at me with a sound like the rush of trains that used to go by our house at night.

Maybe you don't have one day a week to practice Sabbath—I think you should talk to my daughter's rabbi—but maybe you have an hour a day or an hour a week. There are lots of mini-Sabbaths around, if you know where to seek them out.

Here's a slightly different kind of Sabbath.

Several years ago I went canoeing with my friend Robin, who used to work for the Department of Natural Resources. I hate canoeing, because the very idea makes me tired. But Robin lured me onto Lake Pokegama with some promise of visiting a heron marsh and soon I was busy flailing around and feeling like a fool. And getting tired and ready to whine. It was at that moment that Robin gave me a very important piece of information: *rest in the stroke*. He said, "The reason you are getting tired is that you keep your paddle moving all the time. There is an almost imperceptible rest that you have to take at the end of every stroke, and that's where you find the energy to paddle for hours. Rest in the stroke."

This advice doubled my stamina. It also gave me a new way of looking at a lot of physical and metaphysical processes. It's the Garfield school of professional conduct: When can I take a little nap?

It is possible for us to miss lots of naps in the course of the day. Or let's say, moments of rest, moments of vision, moments of beauty. I am capable of working so hard in my garden, whipping down a row of geraniums with my pruning shears that I never see or smell them. Why am I growing them anyway? I am able to walk to class so full of what I'm going to say that I couldn't tell you what kind of day it was. Of teaching with such a fix on ideas that I don't notice who has dyed her hair magenta, or who has a new nose ring. In the Buddhist tradition, practicing mindfulness is the whole point of life: *this* geranium, *this* weather, *this* student. Each moment of attention a little Sabbath.

In struggling over time with the practice of mindfulness, I've discovered that one of the reasons I get so tired out teaching school and living life is that I hold a lot of unnecessary tension in my body, and that it is possible NOT to do that. Let me give you a couple of examples. One of the most hellish times in my day used to be the hour when, as a single parent, I left school, picked up my children from day care, trundled them home, and made supper. My spiritual quest in those days was simply to get food, any food, on the table, and I brought tremendous physical tension to the task. Now when I was at Pendle Hill, that contemplative community I talked about earlier, one of the cooks had a lovely custom. When she was feeling pressured by the demands of feeding fifty people—and each of them would be practicing a different dietary fad—she would light a candle and put it on the table where she worked. Usually this was a raucous kitchen, one that might have a ball game on the radio, or a couple of Swedish fiddlers playing—I don't want to give the impression that it was a pietistical environment. But the candle changed things. It called us to attention.

I brought home the candle custom, and it changed our kitchen, too, though the changes took about five years to effect. I learned to consciously let go of my tension when I lit that candle. I learned to make tamales from scratch. This is no great accomplishment for some people, but I come from an ethnic tradition where it's a big deal to make turnips from scratch. I learned, let me put it this way, the spiritual practice of making tamales from scratch. I came to love the process of stripping the corn out in my garden, of using everything: the corn, the husks, the cobs to steam the little bundles on top of; I loved the feeling of solidarity with the ancient world of women.

Years ago I used to toss hotdogs to children who snapped them up like puppies. Today, by contrast, we practice something we call The Religion of Food and Beauty. My friends constantly tease me about the hours I spend in the kitchen and they tell me how they send out for pizza and how their freezers overflow with frozen dinners—and that's OK, because everybody's idea of rest will be different—but I'm telling you I am *born again* about this Religion of Food and Beauty. Last week we made a cherry pie, from real cherries, that we talked about all week in theological terms.

I am saying, if you don't have time to breathe, if you are run off your feet, try spending twice as much time as you usually spend on a task. It may rest you very nicely. I *try* to light the candle sometimes over my freshman essays (resisting the obvious temptation to set them on fire). It may take me another seven years to establish a religion about this, and by then I'll be ready to retire. But here is one thing I've discovered. I used to spend a lot of energy arguing in absentia with my freshmen and scolding them, which does not promote the tranquil mind. "You dummy, I told you to put your name in the upper left-hand corner. I'll bet you were stoned when you wrote this." And so on; if, by contrast, I cultivate an attitude of friendly visiting as I grade freshman essays—you with the red hair, you with the nose ring—it takes longer but it's twice as restful. And I feel I have done less tearing at the web of life.

My new mantra, then, is "it takes as long as it takes." Some shortcuts complicate life enormously. There's an archetypal Peace Corps story about a young engineer who worked in Africa. He saw the women walking miles every day to the well and decided to help them by digging a well in the village. But when he did so the culture of the village immediately began to decline. The children started to fight. Families stopped speaking to each other. Finally the village picked up its houses and moved two miles away from the new well. That daily walk was essential to shaking out the troubles of the group, offering sympathy and friendship and solutions. I have a young Senegalese friend named Nambe who likes to come to my house for the tamales, and she says, "I just don't understand Americans, they don't take time to make dinner, they don't take time to make love . . ."

Making love and making dinner take time, but they also give you back.

These are sabbaths of spirit: taking the time to ask, "Who am I and what am I doing here?" following, if only for an hour, your intuitions, resting in the stroke, taking twice as much time.

When I was eighteen I started studying yoga with a Catholic monk who stood on his head every day to remind himself that the world could be seen from a different perspective. I have never mastered standing on my head, but I think each of us needs to remind ourselves daily that we are seeing only a very limited reality. The poet William Stafford used to rise every morning at four and write a poem. Somebody said to him, "But surely you can't write a good poem every day, Bill. What happens then?" "Oh," he said, "then I lower my standards." Three great lessons here—practice your art every day, lower your standards, and claim a time or place or an attitude that will challenge the bourgeois idea of reality. Four A.M.! I told this story to my friend Peter, who immediately began getting up at dawn. He called me long distance from Berkeley. "It shakes up your whole soul," he said of that time of day, "it changes things better than Prozac."

The point here is not that you should be getting up at four A.M., but it *is* a bottom-line question: *what are you going to give?* To function as an artist of whatever kind in the academy, or to make tamales from scratch, the sacrifices are big. One of the first and obvious things you might have to put on the line, for example, is academic prestige. But, indeed, each of us might pause here to think about an important piece of self-knowledge we have gained, think about the art we do, or the art we live. Now let us reflect for a moment on what that blessing *cost.* Suppose you met a witch in the woods and she said, "I'll give you self-knowledge, but you have to give me [blankety blank]." Insert here what you gave, blindly or with no choice, or with an overflowing heart, for your best knowledge. With the options presented clearly, as they seldom are in life, most of us would say, *no thanks.*

In Minnesota if you want to be a hardanger fiddler, the old guys will tell you, "Well, you have to go into the woods and when you come to a waterfall, you will hear a *fossegrim*, a kind of troll, playing his violin behind the waterfall. That's where they live. If you apply to the troll for lessons, he will take your fingers and pull them. It will hurt unbearably, but in the end you will be a hardanger fiddler."

So get up at four A.M.; it's an easy way to placate the trolls of art.

Let me conclude with a final koan that seems to have something to do with being an artist. I'll call this story "Somewhere There Is a Great Mystery That Wants to Live in your House and Change Everything." I was out walking, again with my friend Robin, the naturalist, on the university campus near his house. By the side of the road, we came upon a tiny, newborn animal, covered in white hair, eyes closed, moving feebly. Now both Robin and I have raised baby animals pretty successfully, so we paused a long moment to look at this creature. After awhile, as I looked carefully at the contours of its tail, I reached a fatal conclusion. I spent part of my childhood on the East Side of St. Paul, where we do not even *say* a certain word; we spell it, as in "I think I saw an r-a-t in the basement by the drain." On the East Side, we do not like this animal. So I said to Robin, "I think it's an r-a-t." With that piece of labeling we left the animal and walked on.

Later that same evening, I visited my neighbors up the street. This is a minister's family who have for years been famous in the neighborhood for their absolutely fastidious behavior. It's the kind of house where you take off your shoes at the door, where the furniture is covered in plastic, the car is always washed, the bushes are pruned, etc. On this particular evening, as I stopped to pass a few moments, my neighbor the minister wanted to show me the wonderful thing he had literally up his sleeve: their pet squirrel. Now I had heard about this squirrel. In fact the whole neighborhood was talking about it. The family had found it in their yard after a storm—a tiny baby then—and they had been raising it for a year. What the neighbors were saying was, "Do you believe the transformation at the preacher's house? This squirrel has the run of the place. It goes up and down the drapes. It eats from its own little dish at the table. They let it leave its little messes all over and they just laugh." With great pride, the minister showed me his squirrel. Now you see where this story is going. The little animal was enchanting, and tame as a kitten. And as I looked carefully at it, observed the way its ears were set against its skull, the lie of its tail, I knew what I had walked away from earlier in the day.

Or had I? This is a koan. How do we tell a transforming miracle, an angel unaware, from an r-a-t? And would my catalyst for change be the same as the minister's? Surely not, as I need an angel of order rather than an angel of misrule. One of my friends huffily told me, "A squirrel is just a dirty rodent anyway. You're always making everything into a big metaphor." There is no simple moral to this story. It's yours. Take it home if you want to, or let it be.

But *somewhere* there is a great mystery that wants to come live in your house and change everything.

References

Beevers, John. 1975. Introduction. In *Abandonment to Divine Presence*, 9–21. *See* Jean-Pierre de Caussade 1975.

Caussade, Jean-Pierre de. 1975. *Abandonment to Divine Presence*, trans. John Beevers. New York: Image-Doubleday.

Chittister, Joan, O.S.B. 1990. *Wisdom Distilled from the Daily*. New York: Harper and Row.

Dillard, Annie. 1988. *Holy the Firm*. New York: Perennial-Harper.

Douglass, Frederick. 1982. *Narrative of the Life of Frederick Douglass*. New York: Viking Penguin.

Evely, Louis. 1970. *In His Presence*, trans. J. F. Stevenson. New York: Herder and Herder.

Hall, Nor. 1980. *The Moon and the Virgin*. New York: Harper.

Julian of Norwich. 1978. *Julian of Norwich: Showings*, eds. Edmund Colledge, O.S.A. and James Welsh, S.J. New York: Paulist.

Mukherjee, Bharati. 1981. *Jasmine*. New York: Ballantine.

N'hat Hanh, Thich. 1975. *The Miracle of Mindfulness*, trans. Mobi Warren. Boston: Beacon Hill.

Nouwen, Henri. 1981. *The Way of the Heart: Desert Spirituality and Contemporary Ministry*. Minneapolis: The Seabury Press.

Penington, Isaac. 1984. "Selections from the Letters of Isaac Penington." In *Quaker Spirituality*. ed. Douglas V. Steere, 135–157. New York: Paulist.

Rilke, Rainer Maria. 1981. "An Archaic Torso of Apollo." In *Selected Poems of Rainer Maria Rilke*, trans. Robert Bly. 147. New York: Harper.

Stevens, Wallace. 1971. "Esthetique du Mal." In *The Palm at the End of the Mind*, ed. Holly Stevens. 252–263. New York: Random House.

Ueland, Brenda. 1992. "Tell Me More." *Utne Reader* 54(11/12).

Wilbur, Richard. 1988. "Love Calls Us to the Things of This World." In *New and Collected Poems.* 233–234. New York: Harcourt.

Woolman, John. 1989. *The Journal and Major Essays of John Woolman,* ed. Phillips Moulton. Richmond, IN: Friends United.

Wright, James. 1961. "Lying in a Hammock at William Duffy's Farm in Pine Island, Minnesota." In *The Branch Will Not Break,* 16. Middletown, CT: Wesleyan University Press.

Yeats, W. B. 1950. "The Magi." In *The Collected Poems of W. B. Yeats.* 124. New York: Macmillan.